A PUBLIC SCHOOL MIRACLE

Transforming the Hearts and Minds of a School and its Community

Sandra Dean

10-10-10
Publishing

A PUBLIC SCHOOL MIRACLE: Transforming the Hearts and Minds of a School and its Community
www.APublicSchoolMiracle.com
Copyright © 2022 Sandra Dean

Paperback ISBN: 978-1-77277-482-5

References to internet websites (URLs) were accurate at the time of writing. Authors and the publishers are not responsible for URLs that may have expired or changed since the manuscript was prepared.

Limits of Liability and Disclaimer of Warranty
The author and publisher shall not be liable for your misuse of the enclosed material. This book is strictly for informational and educational purposes only.

Warning – Disclaimer
The purpose of this book is to educate and entertain. The author and/or publisher do not guarantee that anyone following these techniques, suggestions, tips, ideas, or strategies will become successful. The author and/or publisher shall have neither liability nor responsibility to anyone with respect to any loss or damage caused, or alleged to be caused, directly or indirectly by the information contained in this book.

Publisher
10-10-10 Publishing
Markham, ON   Canada

Printed in Canada and the United States of America

Second Edition
This book was first published by Penguin Canada in 2000 under the title, *Hearts and Minds - A Public School Miracle.* This manuscript has been revised and updated with new strategies and ideas on leadership and is being published by 10-10-10 Publishing Co under the new title, *A Public School Miracle - Transforming The Hearts and Minds Of A School and its Community.*

To my husband, Ishwar,
If I could choose again, I would choose you.

To my children, Shiva, Lisa, Rishi and Shalini,
and my grandchildren, Nathaniel, Surya,
Joshua, Dante, and Dasha,
You are my inspiration, I love you!

Table of Contents

Foreword

Is the phenomenal success at South Simcoe Public School a miracle?

In some ways, yes, but in grasping what caused the success, we must understand that *A Public School Miracle* is really about 'great leadership,' 'personal and professional growth,' 'finding the good in every person and every situation,' and the science and art of working together to accomplish things that were previously thought to be beyond the reach of humans. It is leadership, team and community building at its best!

This book is full of real children, and the adults who help and harm them. Reading it will elicit a rollercoaster of emotions. The circumstances and actions are described in gut-wrenching reality. But at the same time we see the establishment and persistence of an incredible ability never to confuse symptoms for causes, an unwavering passion, and deeply insightful leadership actions that root out and alter deep causes. South Simcoe literally changed the fortunes of 10-year-olds. This 'public school miracle' is hard headed, and soft hearted in equal measure.

South Simcoe Public School progressed from being the lowest performing school in a district of over 100 schools, to one of the very best; in fact, one of the highest performing schools in the entire province of 4900 schools.

You will not be able to put this book down, and you will never think the same way again about schools in desperate poverty, or what it takes to make them successful. Passion and the unwavering belief that all children, indeed all humans, should and can prosper is foundational, and in order to progress you need a core set of strategies like those Dean and her staff embodied, and instilled in children and adults alike.

Sandra Dean repeatedly shows how a leader's passion and strong values can solve some of the most intractable problems. She created a strong internal team while simultaneously extending the team and 'creating a village' – an extended community of local businesses ranging from the local pizza shop to General Motors.

The journey is beautiful. It starts with being appointed as principal to the worst school in a large district just to the east of Toronto. Sandra's first principle involves the discovery, in fact the uncovering, of personal purpose tied to the particular school and community of which she was a part.

You will discover how to transform your school using real-life strategies gleaned from challenging scenarios. Sandra's principles, such as don't get discouraged in the early going; be transparent about failures and successes; be vulnerable and strong at the same time; never give up; enjoy the small triumphs, but go for even bigger ones; believe in yourself and in the human condition and potential; know that you will win many more than you lose, provide a proven pathway to success.

This award winning school (it won many national and international awards, including one from The Conference Board of Canada, for Excellence in School, Community and Business Partnerships) is a story of success against the odds, a remarkable testimony to the power of human co-operation to achieve remarkable outcomes.

For a long time after 2001, Sandra Dean's work remained an anomaly. It was way ahead of its time. Fast forward two decades and consider South Simcoe with the lens and reality of 2022.

Sandra Dean's Hearts and Minds Model of Leadership™ is what we need in schools and communities today. It is now time for us to revisit this model and implement it in our schools and communities. The conditions are favorable and the need is urgent.

Let us create our modern day miracles!

Michael Fullan, PhD

Acknowledgements

I would like to thank my **parents and grandparents** for always encouraging me to take risks, follow my heart and dream big, and for the love and support they gave to me, and the values they instilled in me as a child.

I deeply appreciate my **mother-in-law** for the wise and wonderful role model that she was.

A special thank you to my siblings and their spouses, **Shirley and Winston, Ranjie and Karen, Naresh and Sue,** for their love, encouragement and support.

Thank you to my professors who became mentors: **Dr. George Phills and Dr. Russell McNeilly.**

I am forever grateful to the children, staff and community of **South Simcoe School,** who worked hand in hand and heart to heart with me as we co-created the "Together We Light the Way" model.

I am honored to have been part of a staff whose dedication and commitment to the children entrusted to their care, was inspiring:

Jane Baier, Doug Beeston, Susan Bickford, Joanne Blohm, Michael Bowman, Vicky Caruana, Dawn Christiansen, Gisele

Cournoyer, Nancy Cregg, Jacki Devolin, Cathie Edwards, Alvena Dunhil, Sara Dunstall, Debbie Faryna, Tamara Gattie, Jennifer Goodbrand, Jane Hallett, Joe Hamilton, Anne Hansen, Trish Horwood, Denise Hoskin, Kim Hutchinson, Kim Whyte, Janet King, Sharon McLean, Heather Morrison, Lona O'Reilly, Claudette Oegema, Annette Parker, Andrea Peel, Jane Pelow, Sally Roberts, Dale Shepphard, Heather Stallaert, Joan Strzelczyk, Anne Taylor, Sandy Thomas, Randy Weekes and Gail Welch.

I deeply appreciate the presidents of the Parent Association, who worked tirelessly to ensure that the "Together We Light the Way" programs and practices would reach many more children: **Roger Morin, Sandra Kanagasabi, Pam and Chris Williams** and **Pat Coles.**

Thank you to my superintendent, **Carol Yeo**, who wouldn't let me leave, and told me I would shine as principal at South Simcoe School.

I am grateful to superintendent **Brian Cain,** who made resources available to me when I had nothing.

I wish to acknowledge the trustees of the Durham District School Board, who all took a special interest in South Simcoe School, and quietly encouraged me in so many ways: **Ian Brown, Louise Farr, Patti Bowman, Marg Jackson, Audrey MacLean, Mike Nicholson, Doug Ross and Kathleen Hopper**, and of course, **Ruth LaFarga**, who sent me to South Simcoe and was always there to guide me.

I would like to thank the Directors of Education: **Ken Munroe**, who gave me such encouragement in my early years as a teacher; **Bruce Mather** for encouraging me to become a school leader; and of course, **Pauline Laing**, who sent me to South Simcoe and quietly and steadfastly supported me all the way through.

I am forever grateful to my mentors—**Don Peel, Chuck Powers, Clarence Prins, Dave Snoddon** and **Doug Wilson**—who were always there to guide me through the rough times.

My thanks to the superintendents who encouraged my work: **Dave Brown, Craig Burch, Casey Daleman, Kaye Egan, Laura Elliot, Bill Fairburn, Bev Freedman, Mike Graham, Doug Kettle, George Marlow, Bob Martin, Jack Massie, Don McLean, Trudy Nisbett** and **Bruce Walker**.

I would like to acknowledge the principals with whom I worked and who encouraged my creativity: **Doug Bell, Jack Gardner, Carmen Sarles, Rodger Lappin, Bob Kochan** and **Bill Kellington**.

I appreciate the counsel and guidance of my colleagues who helped me through many rough times: **Don and Luiga Ayotte, Cathy Barber, Jim Craigen, Rita Edwards, Gail Elliot, Pauline Langmaid, Wendy Peyton, Beth Selby, Dianne Serra, Joan Zamora, Maret Sadem-Thompson,** and **Donna McArthur**.

I thank the Durham Regional Police Service: in particular, **Chiefs Dave Edwards, Trevor McCagherty** and **Kevin McAlpine**; **Deputy Chiefs Bob Jarvest** and **Jim Adams**; Staff Sergeants **Bill**

Temple and Colin Shaw; and the many officers who came to our school and helped us.

Thank you, **Carl Rimar, George Mec** and the Kiwanis Clubs of Oshawa for your dedication to your community.

Many thanks to **Doug Finney** for allowing us to use the Legion Hall for our meetings, since we didn't have a space large enough for all our students to gather. Thank you to the veterans who came to our school to share their stories with our children; they are true heroes.

I wish to thank **Anne Hartling** and **Shoppers Drug Mart** for appreciating the efforts of our students, and displaying the photographs they took in their stores.

Thank you, **Dr. Frank Gold** for being such a kind and wonderful partner.

I am grateful for the assistance of **Barry Kuntz, Tom McNown, Jennifer McDonald** and **Curt Tingley**, from General Motors, who brought their president to visit, worked with my students and invited me to share the South Simcoe story with many of their executives all across Canada.

I deeply appreciate the support and assistance from **Mayor Nancy Diamond** and **Mayor Dan Carter**. They are great role models for students.

Thank you to **Phil Fernandez** from Frontier College, for helping us set up our Circles of Love: Reading Together program.

Thank you, **MPP Jerry Oullette** for always taking the time to drop by the school and encourage us.

I am grateful to the **Conference Board of Canada**, and the people there who awarded, encouraged and supported our efforts: **MaryAnn McLaughlin, Michael Bloom, Linda Scott, Doug Watt** and **Kurtis Kitagawa**.

Thank you to **David Onley, Linda Manjuris, Louise Brown, Gail Gallant, Peter Gzowski, Pat Ganase, Lynne Schuyler** and **Joanne Burghardt**, who highlighted the development of the "Together We Light the Way" model, on TV, radio and in newspaper articles and magazines.

I appreciate everything I learned from **Carol Slater** (O.I.S.E. University of Toronto) and **Allison Griffith** (York University), my two principals at the principal's courses. They gave me the opportunity to develop the courses and be a part of an outstanding group of school leaders.

I would like to thank Professors **Michael Fullan, Andy Hargreaves and Ken Leithwood**, whose research formed the foundation for the programs and strategies we implemented at South Simcoe School.

I deeply appreciate the guidance of **Courtney Garneau**, who heard me being interviewed by **Peter Gsowski** on CBC Radio, and asked me to come to Ottawa. This led to our grant from the federal government. We were asked to develop a Canadian model for school and community success.

I would like to acknowledge my advisers at the Federal Department of Justice: **Michel Vallee, Patricia Begin, Greg McDougall, Dana Donovan, Audrey Lorimer, Monty Pitson** and

For The Hearts and Minds Leadership™ resources go to ...

Lucy Leonard, who supervised the project and provided opportunities for it to be shared in Australia, China, Thailand and at the O.E.C.D. in Paris.

I would like to thank my project advisors: **Eric Newell, Roland Hosein, Bob Ellis, Ken Leithwood** and **Linda Sinclair**. They were there, every time I needed assistance.

Many thanks to **Rob Pitfield** from Scotiabank, for being a sounding board, a cheerleader and for funding my work in the Caribbean.

A huge thank you to CEO **Bob Gillespie**, V.P. **Roland Hosein**, V.P. **Bob Weese** and the G.E. Foundation for their generous multi-year funding of the project.

I would like to acknowledge the International Partnership Network—in particular, **Chris and Carol Lea, Gordon McKay, Betsy Nelson and Alex Blackwood**—for the opportunities they gave me to present the "Together We Light the Way" model in Norway, Scotland, England, South Africa, India and Brazil.

I am so thankful to the wonderful people who helped me to transition from the school to the district office, take the programs and practices we had developed at the school and create the materials to help other schools to implement them: **Roxanne Brown, Brenda Cannon, Mark Joel, Marlene Gutsole, Mike Lancaster, Andrea Peel** and **Kim Whyte**.

I would like to thank **Daphne Hart**, my literary agent, who called and asked me to write a book about South Simcoe School; as well as **Lynne Schuyler**, from Reader's Digest, and **Cynthia**

Good, Jackie Kaiser and Barbara Berson, from Penguin Press, for convincing me there was a book.

I deeply appreciate the assistance of **Peter Edwards** and **John Reynolds**, two talented writers who helped me to tell my story.

I would also like to thank the people at Sifton for the beautiful home I write in: **Donna Czack, Gabi Brown, Paul Matte, Georgia Murray, Ken Oudshoorn, Barb Owens, Brittany Ready,** and last but not least, **Scott White.**

With deep appreciation to **Nancy Levin, Kathe Crawford, Holly Messick** and **Linda Perry**, for assisting me to step out of my grief and back into life, after the death of my beloved husband.

I would like to acknowledge my publisher, **Raymond Aaron**, and the 10 10 10 publishing group: **Mikee Patel, Christina Fife, Danielle Stevens, Chinmai Swamy** and **Liz Ventrella.**

I extend a huge thank you to Director **Grant Yeo**, Superintendent **Norm Powers** and parent **Roger Morin**, who gave me the courage and assistance to get this book written.

Last but not least, I would like to thank **Michael Bowman, Linda Lopeke** and **Ann Marie Luce,** whose assistance and support helped me to get this new edition completed. I am so grateful to them.

A Message to the Reader

The children you will read about in this book are unique, as are all children; their experiences and achievements are theirs alone. But they have something in common with your own children, your neighbors' children and children living elsewhere in your community—this is vital to your understanding and appreciation of the story about to unfold on the following pages.

The children in your family and your neighborhood may not endure the trials faced by many of the boys and girls whose stories you are about to encounter. Those to whom you are closest may be—and I pray they are—free from physical and emotional abuse, confident in the love and support of their families and enjoying a life of comfort and good health. Yet they, just like the students from South Simcoe, are vulnerable, impressionable and struggling to understand and assume their role in their community.

Both these children and those in your own neighborhood will eventually assume responsibilities as adults. That is their common destiny. They will be your physician, your visiting homemaker, your care-giver and protector, your hope and trust for the future. In other words, their eventual role is to help you, and your current role is to assist them in meeting the challenges of being a child.

During the years I served as principal of South Simcoe Public School, I was privileged to spend time at what I do best and love most: teaching and working with children. I was also fortunate to do so with a dedicated team who shared my concern and commitment, and with community partners who gave generously of their time and their love. Together, our efforts helped the students of South Simcoe Public School to become more resilient and successful.

The children of South Simcoe are not the only ones who needed this encouragement to use their voice in their own society. The need exists among all children everywhere. It is a need that all of us should be prepared to fulfill with enthusiasm, with dedication and with love. This is the message of South Simcoe Public School.

What Happened After I Left the School

The decision to leave my position as principal, in order to document and transfer the Together We Light the Way programs and practices to other schools, communities and countries, was not an easy one for me. In fact, it was a downright scary proposition. What did I know about leading this type of initiative?

Kanta and Om Arora, Paula Daniel, Courtney Garneau, Roland Hosein, Ken Leithwood, Roger Morin, Eric Newell, Rob Pitfield, Colin Shaw, Carol Shepherd, Linda Sinclair, Wendy Sokoloff and so many other supporters promised that they would guide and support me as I moved forward, and I leaned heavily on them during the following years.

Our project, Creating Safe and Caring Learning Communities, using our Together We Light the Way programs and practices, was implemented in many schools and communities across Canada and beyond.

Presentations were made, and training was conducted in several countries: Australia, Brazil, China, Egypt, England, France, Grenada, India, Jamaica, Norway, Scotland, South Africa, Spain, Thailand, and Trinidad and Tobago. In the U.S.A., we were invited to "testify" at the White House Initiative on Hispanic American Affairs. Later, we were asked to make a presentation at the OECD's (Organization for Economic Co-operation and Development) headquarters in a beautiful and impressive French Chateau.

This organization's work on education helps individuals and nations to identify and develop the knowledge and skills that drive better jobs and better lives, generate prosperity and promote social inclusion. All of this was to show an example of how a school and its community can work together to strengthen each other, contribute to the development of its young citizens and help to create social cohesion. Together We

Light the Way was used as a Canadian model for others to follow at the launch of the International Bullying Network in Norway, hosted by the OECD and the Norwegian government.

Yes, South Simcoe School was closed, but the funding from the Federal government of Canada, the Ontario government, the GE Foundation, and Scotiabank, ensured that its teachings live on. Through seminars, workshops, program trainings and our wonderful student graduates, South Simcoe School continues to Light The Way.

Chapter 1

A Dream Fulfilled

The thing I remember most clearly is the strange instance of silence just before my heart leaped at the news.

In that fraction of time, everything crystallized for me: the hopes, the frustrations and the memories of so many tears and, yes, so much laughter too. During that brief moment, they all became real again, and the crises and tragedies that often accompanied them were nowhere in sight.

Then the screaming and the shouting started—nineteen educators, two police officers and one director of education, all of us a thousand miles from home, leaping on the spot, holding hands, hugging and laughing, while others in the hall smiled with pleasure at our unbridled joy.

It was April 1995, and South Simcoe Public School, which three years earlier had suffered the humiliation of having the worst student marks of all the schools in the region, had just won a national award for "Excellence in Business and Education Partnerships," from the Conference Board of Canada. What's more, the travel expenses for the staff members who attended the ceremony in Saint John, New Brunswick, had been paid for by donations from business partners who believed in us, supported our work, and wanted to provide an opportunity for as many teachers as possible to participate in the celebration.

But I wasn't thinking of that as we all crowded onto the platform to accept the prize and acknowledge the standing ovation from the audience. No academy award-winning celebrities could ever have felt a greater thrill of accomplishment than we did at that moment. We had managed to prove something vital about education; first to ourselves, then to our students, their parents and the community, and now to the entire country and beyond.

How far we have come, I thought, watching the staff celebrate that evening in Saint John. We had so far to travel from that first day, and by taking small steps and staying on the path, we arrived at our destination.

Becoming principal of my own school had been a dream of mine almost from the first day I chose teaching as a career. It's not an unusual ambition, I suspect. Every teacher dedicated to making a positive impact on students, and prepared to challenge the usual way of doing things, thinks from time to time about being appointed principal. In early 1991, the position was offered to me. However, when I discovered that my school would not be a neat and tidy suburban one, furnished with shining facilities and peopled by solidly middle-class students, but a tired, seventy-five-year-old inner-city school that probably faced closure, I admit my heart sank a little.

Built when schools were considered part monument and part institution, the structure was small and dark, its brown brick walls crowned with stone and concrete in a style that reminded me of pictures of Queen Victoria staring at the camera, stern and forbidding.

Its location, directly across the street from a strip mall, was a principal's nightmare. The teachers at South Simcoe faced enormous difficulties as a result of these and other factors. The proof was in the test scores. Of all schools in the Durham District School Board, South Simcoe Public School ranked last when it came to measuring student performance levels in reading, writing and mathematics.

Yet, within a short number of years, South Simcoe Public School would rise to the top of all schools in its district. Not just higher, or among the best of its group, or even among the top ten, it would sit at the very summit, with 100 percent of its students performing at the highest levels in the same subjects in which it had scored poorest.

This is the story of its journey from last to first. It was not always smooth or swift, and from time to time we encountered a pothole or two along the way. But oh, how rewarding the trip was for everyone...especially our students!

When I first learned that I would be stepping up to the role of principal at a school within my district, I was naturally pleased and excited. Promotion to a principal is more than recognition of your professional abilities and experience; it's an unrivalled opportunity to influence your students' future in a manner no other profession can offer. As a parent, you are a lifelong influence on your own children's lives; as a teacher, you affect the lives of perhaps twenty-five or thirty children in your care each day. But as a principal, you have the opportunity to make a positive impact on literally hundreds of children, and improve their lives in at least some small way. Me, a principal? I could hardly wait to get started. Just tell me where!

To say that I had mixed emotions when the answer came back "South Simcoe Public School," is something of an understatement. In fact, my first reaction was immediately negative. "I don't want to go there," I said to my superintendent, Carol, when she called me at home with the news. For as long as anyone could remember, South Simcoe was located on the "wrong side of the tracks." This is more than a cliché in industrial Oshawa, where economic and social conditions are clearly stratified. "It's an old school; they're going to close it soon, and it's not my kind of place." Those were three pretty good reasons to send somebody else, I believed.

"Sandra, South Simcoe is your kind of place," Carol replied. "The students need someone like you. You can make a real difference there. Look, I promise you, if you go there, you'll shine." She must have sensed that I remained unconvinced, because she added, "If, in a few months, you still feel you would rather go somewhere else, we'll talk about it." Naturally, I agreed. I really wanted to be a principal, after all.

One of the things all educators discover is that you never stop learning. There are lessons to be gained from virtually everything you experience as a teacher and as a school leader. Certainly, over my seven and a half years as principal of South Simcoe Public School, I absorbed many lessons, and the first came from my own family on the very day I was told of my appointment.

"We're so proud of you," my husband, Ishwar, said. My sons, Shiva and Rishi, along with other family members, added their congratulations. But the expression on my face, and my own self-doubts, became immediately apparent.

"I'm not sure I can handle it," was my reply. The truth was, I felt more than doubt; I felt disappointment as well. Like every profession, teaching has its share of prestigious positions, and being principal of a school like South Simcoe was not one of them.

"Of course you can," Ishwar said. "You'll make a great principal. You have the training, the experience and, most of all, the attitude to deal with students who need extra care, love and attention. It's the best place for you."

"It's kind of dreary," I said. "You know how those older school buildings are; not much light, dull colors, huge hallways…

"Then we'll help you fix things up," Ishwar said. "The boys and I will pitch in before the school year starts. A little paint and some wallpaper can make a big difference; you know that." He added, in a more serious tone, "Besides, it's not the building that needs your talents; it's the students."

This initial lesson, of course, taught me that I wasn't alone. I enjoyed the total support of my family, and the support base grew over the years to encompass first the school staff and then the parents, local merchants, service clubs, the police department and finally the entire community. Ishwar was absolutely correct. I was not alone, and in no way could I have accomplished as much as I did without the support of this ever-widening circle of people who worked with me to make a difference.

Many of my beliefs about raising and educating children are hardly new, such as the idea that children are to be valued and nurtured in order to bring out the best in them. Their precious spirit stems, in my opinion, from all their potential within and their open hearts. We all know that these two qualities are often dulled with the passage of time and the experience of living; some say that's part of the process of maturing into an adult. So many children lose them too early and in the wrong way—some through abuse, neglect and the oppression of social conditions; others through parental and societal expectations and so much more.

I have yet to encounter a troubled child who could not benefit from healthy doses of love and care. For some reason, a few members of our society believe that individuals in the two extremes of life—childhood and old age—either don't require or don't deserve our full attention. How can this be? Why can't children enjoy the same degree of dignity and respect that we demand for ourselves? Imagine for a moment that you are no longer as independent as you are today. You can be either a child or an elderly invalid—it works either way—and you are under the control of someone stronger than yourself, someone who seeks to dominate you with threats and punishment. How would you feel?

Control and manipulation of children are ultimately doomed to failure. I saw proof of this during my years of teaching, in my position as vice-principal and, of course, in my experience as a parent. I sincerely believe that the best method of educating children is, first, to appreciate that they came into this world filled with potential, with gifts, talents and capabilities to be uncovered; and then to believe in them and all that they are capable of doing, and who they are capable of becoming. Then love them, care for them, nurture and guide them, and help them to build a strong sense of themselves. With this mental and emotional foundation in place, we need to provide them with opportunities to experience the joy and deep sense of personal satisfaction that comes from accomplishing something and doing it well.

You don't teach a child to ice-skate, for example, by threatening punishment if she doesn't learn how to keep her ankles stiff. You demonstrate and encourage. You praise and support. You do not threaten. And when you experience the delight on a child's face when she finally masters such a skill, you share in her pleasure, pride and sense of accomplishment.

Does this mean that any behavior is acceptable from children? Of course not. As adults, we recognize our responsibility as members of society. Physical assaults, theft, disturbances, hurting and harming others in any way are simply not acceptable. But neither, I believe, should they be dealt with simply by punishment. There are quick and easy consequences that may seem to be a solution, but they are not a long-term one; it isn't that easy. It is never that easy, as almost anyone in our justice system will agree.

These ideas represented the core of my beliefs, which I mulled over as I prepared myself to assume the role of principal at South Simcoe Public School, the first step in a journey that led to all the whooping and excitement in New Brunswick and beyond.

Looking back on it, I realize that my career could have taken one of two very different routes. The one that I originally longed to travel would have been smooth and paved, across generally flat terrain. I would have followed this route as principal of a bright and shiny school in a wealthy suburb, a school populated by students whose minds were filled as much (or, let's face it, more!) with visions of new fashions and the sounds of new music as with the lessons at hand. Such a journey would require little passion and energy from me.

The other route was uncertain and rocky, traversing new territory and climbing from a deep valley up steep canyon walls, ever upwards, stumbling from time to time, with the ever-present risk of falling to disaster. Finishing the trek would test my abilities as an educator, and my strengths as a person, and require large reserves of nerve, energy and belief in myself. In addition, this was not something I could do by myself; I would need an entire team to work with me. But at the end, if we succeeded, we would all stand higher and prouder than when we began. We would leave a legacy that would benefit others for years to come.

That's the route I took when I agreed to become principal of South Simcoe Public School. I did it because I knew I had the support of my family, my friends, my colleagues and my school district.

"Did I do something wrong?" I asked Ruth Lafarga, the day after I learned I had been assigned to South Simcoe School. Ruth chaired the school board and was the elected trustee of the area that included the school. As much as anyone, she knew the challenges facing South Simcoe and me.

"No, of course not," she said laughing. "We want someone like you there to turn things around."

That was my second lesson. I wasn't being sent to South Simcoe merely out of convenience. I was being sent there to turn the school around, by people who believed in my abilities. This was a challenge that would put all my professional skills and capabilities, as well as my personal values and beliefs, to the test. It was a place where I could do a lot of good for many people.

Well, I thought, hanging up the telephone, we might as well get started.

What do you believe about educating children?
What legacy do you wish to create?
If you feel you are ready to start creating
a powerful legacy in your life and career, let's get connected,
please go to my website: APublicSchoolMiracle.com.

Chapter 2

Discovering My Purpose

When I am asked about the source of the ideas and concepts we used at South Simcoe Public School, I realize that many of them have their roots in my experiences growing up in Trinidad, and most were a part of me by the time I was ten years old.

Trinidad is a country similar to Canada in some ways, yet very different in others. The climate and geography of the two countries could not be more different, and the total area of Trinidad and Tobago is much less than that of Prince Edward Island, Canada's smallest province.

Perhaps as a result of the warm and sunny climate, people in Trinidad and other Caribbean islands find it natural to extend their hand to others without being asked. I loved living in this environment as a child, and when I became an educator, I wanted to recreate the village environment and the extended-family concept for the students in my care.

My clearest childhood memories in Trinidad are of my father, who actively sought out those who were in need, and found a way to provide assistance. Instead of waiting to be asked for help, he would travel to villages far beyond our own city, looking for ways he could make people's lives easier.

As a young child, I often accompanied my father on these journeys, and I was continuously struck by the difference between the lives of those he encountered and my own. Our family was middle class. We enjoyed luxuries and never wanted for food, shelter or security. Meeting people who were desperately in need of support, and watching my father find ways to help solve their problems, made him something of a miracle worker in my eyes.

When I asked my father why some of these people did not have enough to eat or a comfortable place to live, as we did, he explained that they had no money to purchase those things.

"Why don't they just go out and make the money they need?" I asked.

"That is not always as easy as it sounds. They need help to be able to do that, which is why I try to help them," my father explained, "so that they can find ways of improving their existence."

It was a simple and honest response, but an important one to me. My father did not believe in simple handouts of food and other items, from those, such as our own family, who had resources to share. Gifts to those in need were important of course, but he wanted to help people learn how to help themselves, and take responsibility for themselves. He knew this was the way to help them to create new lives for themselves and their families. I have never met anyone who takes pride in being handed food, money or clothing, and then being sent away. And I have never failed to notice the pleasure felt by people, especially children, when they achieve something that they and others once believed was beyond their reach. That feeling of accomplishment and success lasts longer than any handout, and can literally change people forever. I was impressed by my father's concern for others because it made me realize how fortunate our family was in many ways. As the eldest child in our family, I may have been the most privileged of all.

The significance of family ties, and the importance of education, reigned supreme in our house. Our ancestors had emigrated to Trinidad from India, where wisdom, knowledge and compassion were considered among the greatest treasures anyone could acquire. They arrived in the mid-nineteenth century, after slavery had been abolished on the island and new labor was needed to harvest the sugar crops. Even as fieldworkers, they retained an appreciation for the value of education, and a respect for the wisdom gained over a lifetime.

I was continually reminded of the importance of education by my grandmother, who, ironically, never attended school (which I realize now was a lesson in itself). Although her father and brothers were well educated (her father had arrived from India as a court interpreter), she had never been to school. During her childhood years, education for girls had been considered a waste. Beyond knowing how to sew, cook, clean

13

house and raise children, what other skills did a woman need? That was how many people thought in the early twentieth century. In quiet rebellion, my grandmother taught herself to count, a skill she used when selling vegetables from the small garden she planted and tended, and she expected all her grandchildren, boys and girls alike, to obtain all the education they could absorb.

In my grandmother's view, living a good life, being kind, helping others, education and happiness, were all intertwined. "You have to ask yourself why you are on this earth," she would tell us. "We are all here to do something special. You've got to get a good education, discover your purpose and, in a loving and kind way, work to make your dreams come true; this will bring you peace and true happiness.

I spent my early school days in a private convent school, where the teaching nuns were kind and caring, creating a sense of family among us. The sisters had high expectations for their students, and firmly instilled in us the need to use self-regulation and self-accountability strategies. If something needed to be done by a certain time, at a certain level of skill, we were expected to find a way to achieve it. If we did not, we were encouraged to keep trying, ask for help if needed and not simply give up. We knew that they were always there to support us. There were times when the other students and I doubted our ability to do something, whether mastering a new algebra method or completing a reading assignment. But the sisters were always convinced that we were worthy and capable, and they managed to pass this belief on to us. I cannot overemphasize the value of this lesson to a child, even a child such as myself, who was constantly being told by my parents that I could achieve anything I wanted to once I committed my heart and mind to it. It is important for everyone—parents, teachers and the entire community—to believe in the potential of children.

For our twenty-fifth wedding anniversary, Ishwar and I travelled to France. There I met my retired school principal, Sister Marie Joseph, who had taken a special interest in me back at that convent school in Trinidad. I wanted to let her know how much she had influenced me, and how many of my successes owed their beginnings to her interest in me. She had encouraged me to read all kinds of books, not just for knowledge but for the sheer joy of reading. She introduced me to *The Good Earth,* by Pearl S. Buck, and to Nancy Drew! She had made me feel good about myself as a student and as an individual, and encouraged me to be courageous and take risks. She was kind and caring, and while I don't know if I meant any more to her than anyone else, *I felt that I did.* I knew that she believed in me, valued me as a person as well as a student, and that I had a place in her heart, *and it made all the difference to me and who I have become.* That was why, so many years after I left the convent school, I wanted to see her again. I wanted her to see that her trust and belief had not been misplaced in me. I went to France to do it. I would have travelled much farther if I had to.

I was taught to value education; it is like a treasure in your mind, and it never loses its value. Knowledge enables you to think for yourself, take care of yourself and help others. This idea of a treasure you carry in your own head is probably why a lot of families in Trinidad aspired to higher education—because it has a value of its own that can never fade.

At home, my parents had high expectations for us, both for academics and behavior. They never allowed anything to intrude seriously on our education. If we had a school test, or an assignment to complete for the following day, our family would not plan a social event for that evening. School work came first, and that was that.

Family ties in Trinidad are extensive and powerful, and we saw our extended family members on weekends. Socializing is not something you do to pass the time or fulfill an obligation. It is as much a part of your life as the work you perform—perhaps more so.

Socializing began with our immediate family. My mother insisted on all of us eating a nutritious breakfast and enjoying healthy meals during the day. We were always expected to eat together, sharing stories of our day with one another across the dinner table. Naturally, holidays were celebrated with great joy and much tradition. On Christmas Day, my father and his four brothers would visit their grandmother with all of us—children, grandchildren and even great-great-grandchildren in later years.

These were wonderful times. We shared news and gossip, each of us knowing that we enjoyed mutual love and support.

And it wasn't a one-way street between the generations. My grandmother travelled regularly, spending a week with each of her children and grandchildren, ensuring everyone was all right. She even visited me in Canada when my son Rishi was born; she spent several weeks with me and her newest great grandchild to help me adjust and get settled into a new routine, as much as to let me know she loved and cared about me. It's the kind of thing mothers and grandmothers did in our family. Her journeys reflected the same kind of attitude my father displayed when he reached out to see who needed assistance in a far-off village. You didn't wait for someone to arrive on your doorstep pleading for help; you went looking for ways to help others.

There were other lessons to be learned as well. I remember one year when, as a young girl, I discovered a special fascination for dolls. I wanted not just ordinary dolls but *special* dolls—large and lifelike, dressed in fancy clothing. One Christmas, I received just such a doll from my parents, and I thought it was the most fabulous of its kind in all of Trinidad.

That same Christmas, a visitor to our home brought his visiting brother along to meet us. Friends and family always made a point of visiting during the Christmas season, and tradition held that visitors were always welcome to bring friends or relatives with them to share the joy of the season. The brother was kind enough to bring a gift for me.

When I unwrapped the gift in front of the visitor, I discovered it was a doll. The doll was pleasant enough, but it couldn't compare with the large, elaborate doll my parents had given me. "Oh," I said, "another doll; thank you," and I set it aside.

My mother immediately suggested I come to the kitchen to assist her with the meal preparation. Of course, she didn't need my help at all. I was the one in need—of a lesson.

"That young man took a lot of time and put a lot of care into choosing that doll for you," she said, after setting me down in a chair. "He told me that he wanted you to have a special gift. You should accept it with the same amount of love and care he put into selecting it for you. So when you go back into the room, you need to pick up the doll, walk over to him, thank him for it and find something good to say about it."

I think I may have pouted a little. "But it's not as nice as my other dolls," I said. "I don't like it."

"I know you can find something good to say about the doll," she told me. "Look carefully at it until you do. Then you go and thank him for it properly, and give him a hug to show you mean it."

As usual, my mother was pleasant but firm. So I returned to the living room and examined the doll more closely. The hair, I saw, was all curly and shiny and actually quite pretty. I took the doll over to our guest and said, "Thank you for my doll. I really like her curly hair."

His reaction was immediate. His eyes lit up with joy and he

reached out to hug me. "I'm so glad you like it," he said. "I was so afraid that I might choose a gift for you that you didn't like."

I have never forgotten the feeling this gave me. Or the lessons it taught me. I learned that all gifts should be received with gratitude and love, and that we must avoid hurting people's feelings; instead, we should always leave them with their dignity intact, feeling cared for and respected. I learned that guests in our home should be treated with courtesy and kindness. I also learned that, if you take the time to truly look, you will discover beauty in things that you may at first have thought to be ordinary. With the right mindset, you can "find the good" in anything and any situation.

Childhood is filled with such lessons. I was fortunate because virtually all of my lessons were positive ones, and I am often surprised at how many I was able to apply when teaching. The lessons include:

Family and good friends make everyone emotionally strong. Look after those who do not have their own; include them with yours.

Children are precious gifts. They are filled with limitless potential, goodness, love and joy. Nurture them, support them, care about them, believe in them and, above all, love them, as they learn, grow, develop and blossom into their true essence and find their paths.

Everyone is unique and has a role to play in moving the world forward. Know that you are unique and special, and therefore have a unique role to play. We are all like a large family, like a giant puzzle that needs all the pieces in order to be complete. One person is no more or no less important than another.

Everyone has strengths, gifts, talents and capabilities that they carry within. Believe in yourself, and know that you are worthy and of value. Believe in others, and understand that everyone is worthy and has value.

Everyone has the right to be respected, and with that right comes the responsibility to respect others. Accept this and act accordingly. Respect yourself, and act with caring, kindness, respect and love. Remember that everything you do—every thought, every word, every small gesture, every act you perform—creates a ripple and affects others. Always be loving, caring, compassionate, kind and respectful.

Give a gift of love and kindness every day. Reach out and do something to help others. Serving others brings great joy and happiness to them, and fulfillment to yourself.

For most of my life, I probably did not analyze these lessons in this manner; I simply applied them from habit. But that's the point: they were so deeply rooted in me that I cannot be separated from these values, any more than I can be separated from a part of my body. This helped me to help other parents and teachers understand the importance of understanding what your values and beliefs are, how they guide the decisions and choices that you make and the actions you take, and how they define you as an individual.

These lessons would prove just as valid to the students of South Simcoe Public School as they did to me. We used them as a starting point for creating our Hearts and Minds Guiding Principles, and our vision, which served as a compass for all our efforts. Applying them to all that we did made a remarkable difference for our students.

Go to my website to download a full color, full size, print ready copy of the Guiding Principles for The Hearts and Minds Leadership Model.™

GUIDING PRINCIPLES
HEARTS AND MINDS LEADERSHIP
AWAKEN TO YOUR UNIQUENESS AND BECOME THE LEADER YOU WERE MEANT TO BE™

Contribution
Everyone is significant and has a contribution to make.

Assets
Everyone has strengths which must be nurtured and supported.

Rights and responsibilities
We all have the right to be respected, and we all have a responsibility to be respectful to others.

Everyone
Everyone is unique and has a role to play.

Service to others, performed with CARE™ and love, leaves a legacy in the heart as well as the mind.

AWAKEN LEAD SERVE

At age nineteen, my life changed in three significant ways: I graduated from the University of the West Indies, with a degree in sociology and political science; Ishwar and I were married; and we emigrated to Canada—all within a few exciting months.

Ishwar was doing graduate work in physics at the University of Western Ontario, in London, Ontario. The special atmosphere of a university campus made our transition from Trinidadian to Canadian life a little easier, because so many people we encountered on the university campus were also from somewhere else and making the same adjustments.

We were not looking forward to our first Christmas away from our families; we missed them very much. Then our new friends, George and Acklema Phills, welcomed us into their fold and invited us to spend Christmas day with them, so that we would still experience a sense of family. Their warmth and kindness, and the beauty of the first heavy snowfall, helped to create a foundation for this new phase of our lives.

The birth of our two sons quickly plunged me into all the activities of motherhood. Things changed, of course, often in ways I did not immediately recognize. Until then, I had had little interest in furthering my education. But the sight of my children playing, sleeping, yearning to learn and reacting to life itself, sparked something in me. I realized that I did want to pursue a career, and that I wanted to make a difference, not just to my children but also to others, in the same manner that many people made a difference to me as a child.

I felt deep in my heart that I should become a teacher. I was especially drawn to the idea of teaching young children who were hampered with learning difficulties of some kind. I knew that the biggest changes were often made during the earliest years, and that children with learning difficulties needed a special kind of help.

Incidentally, becoming a teacher after earning a degree in sociology and political science is not as much of a leap as some people may think. My social and political studies had reaffirmed my beliefs about engaging people and helping them to help themselves.

I could be a voice for underprivileged students and help them be successful. So, with the enthusiastic support of my husband, I obtained my post graduate teaching qualifications and began my career working with autistic children. From there, I progressed through a series of public schools until, by 1989, I had achieved vice-principal status at Glen Dhu Public School, a brand new school in an affluent area of Whitby, Ontario, about thirty miles east of Toronto.

Around the same time, I began teaching the principal's course at the University of Toronto's Ontario Institute for Studies in Education (OISE), and later at York University. These leadership sessions, on evenings, weekends and during the summer months, helped me maintain a wider view of the challenges of education, especially from the perspective of a school leader.

This helped me avoid getting caught up in the day-to-day challenges at my school, and becoming frustrated and thinking that everything that went wrong was because of me. It wasn't about me. It also helped me to keep abreast of the ongoing research on learning and schooling, and I was careful to take all of this into consideration when making changes at South Simcoe Public School.

"You should be a principal," my husband would frequently suggest to me. I would reply that I certainly hoped to be, someday. "Then I'll be able to make a difference for so many more students," I would add.

Only when I discovered that my long-dreamed-of appointment was to be principal of South Simcoe Public School, did my confidence waver. "Be careful about what you wish for," I recalled having read years earlier, "because it may come true."

Well, my wish had come true, in a sense. Now I had to prove I really wanted it—prove it to my family, my staff, the district officials who recommended me and, most of all, to myself.

How do you view your role as a school leader?
Are you ready to play a bigger role in your school and community? If you are then contact me at APublicSchoolMiracle.com.

Chapter 3

A Healthy, Safe and Loving Place for Learning

As familiar as I was with South Simcoe Public School and the challenges faced by its staff and students, I had never set foot inside the building. When, among the many congratulatory messages I received, one came from Wendy, the woman I was replacing as principal, I quickly accepted her invitation to visit.

The steady roar of traffic, speeding west to Toronto and east towards Montreal on nearby Highway 401, is a constant reminder of the transient nature of the South Simcoe neighborhood. And it is not just the traffic that is constantly in motion. About half of the families whose children attended the school, moved in or out of the area each year, an astonishing rate of turnover.

Whatever the reasons for this steady migration, and there were several, the effect on young children of this repeated coming and going of neighbors and friends was often devastating. Add the familiar problems of other inner-city schools, such as family disintegration, high unemployment, spousal abuse, drug and alcohol abuse and more, and it's no surprise that the local public school was often a maelstrom of rebellion, aggression, vandalism and failed dreams.

The building itself seemed to reflect the despair. The square, brown-brick building squatted on a low, bare rise. I remember especially the barren ground and the peeling paint on the window frames. When built in 1916, South Simcoe Public School had sat amid the homes of proud factory workers, many of them recent immigrants employed at the giant General Motors automotive plant.

Over the decades since, most of the more stable families abandoned the area in favor of middle class suburban comfort. As a result, property values nosedived, and many homes in the area became stopovers for transient families.

The school became more than a casualty and a symptom of this decline. From the outside, South Simcoe Public School held little promise that anything positive could happen beneath its roof.

I left my car within sight of several bored teenagers, who were smoking in the mall directly across the street. Inside, the school maintained its rather sad appearance. Much of it was due, of course, to the old building's basic structure, dating back to a much earlier period of architectural design and educational environment. The school's library was miniscule, and as for the gymnasium—well, there *was* no gymnasium, and that was that. The staff room was in the basement, in a converted coal bunker, and just to make things more annoying, the only staff washroom was up three flights of stairs.

My attention was quickly diverted from the building to the students. I had developed the habit of always smiling at children, in my roles as teacher and vice-principal. It put them at ease and helped dissolve the barriers created between students and staff. When I smiled at the children I passed on my way to the principal's office, the smiles I received back from them were more spontaneous and intense than I had become accustomed to at my suburban school. Their entire faces seemed to light up, as though they had been waiting for me to arrive and express pleasure at seeing them.

Naturally, I couldn't help commenting on it when Wendy graciously welcomed me into the school and escorted me into her office. She wasn't surprised at my reaction.

"The kids here are truly wonderful," she told me. "They appreciate every bit of attention you give them, and that's what keeps me going some days."

Of all the discoveries I made that day, her comment about the need of these children for attention and support was the most encouraging. You can't, after all, blame a community for the troubles that occur in and around it. Nor can you blame a teaching staff faced with the challenge of teaching children whose minds may be diverted by empty stomachs, strife between their parents, neglect and abuse.

The fact is, I didn't believe in placing blame at all. Blame would not help me to provide the children with breakfast, resolve their insecurity and fear of failure, or comfort them when the world seemed hostile and unforgiving. It is an essentially useless exercise, a waste of energy and time. I hadn't been sent there to do that, I knew. I was there to do the best job I could for the children, and the brilliance of the smiles I received on my way to the principal's office made me more determined than ever to achieve my goal.

During the rest of the day, I chatted one-on-one with the teachers at South Simcoe, and discovered, to my surprise, that most of them enjoyed their time at the school. Sure, the old building was inefficient, even depressing sometimes. And creating a bond with parents was especially difficult because so many families moved in and out of the neighborhood so often, and those who remained, frequently did not feel confident enough in their own academic skills to help their children with homework and projects.

"Then what is it that gives you so much enjoyment here?" I kept asking, and over and over the answer came back: "The children."

I left South Simcoe convinced that by working with these people, we could make a difference. I knew that I had the support of my family, my friends and the school board officials who sent me there, plus my years of training and experience. The most encouraging thing was that I would be helping the children whose needs were so compelling that I felt I simply *must* apply my very best efforts to make a difference for them.

I was no longer dwelling on the question of whether my appointment to South Simcoe was a good thing or a bad thing. I was no longer hearing those voices. Instead, I was hearing my father's voice. "Don't wait for others to ask for help," I could hear him saying. "Reach out and help them."

And my grandmother's voice echoed as well. *"We are all here to do something special. You've got to discover your purpose and, in a loving and kind way, work to make your dreams come true; this will bring you peace, joy and true happiness.*

I realized, though, that all my training and good intentions would not be enough to change South Simcoe into the kind of school I envisioned; I needed help. I spent a great deal of time researching reference material on inner-city schools, guided by Professor Ken Leithwood, a friend and mentor from the Ontario Institute for Studies in Education at the University of Toronto. As we quickly discovered, the problems of inner-city schools in Canada, and the impact of trauma on children, were well documented by statistics.

We also uncovered much general information on education problems experienced by students in these situations, and the impact of poverty and domestic conflict on society as a whole. But at the time, there was very little written on what to do to solve the problems that came into the classrooms as a result of these situations, or best practices and Canadian success stories that we could learn from and use as models.

I moved from the general to the specific: What could I discover about South Simcoe from its records? The answer was devastating and, once again, my roller coaster ride of emotions took a nosedive.

Poring over records provided by the previous principal, I discovered that the attendance rates for South Simcoe Public School were disappointing, as were the academic scores of its students—although, on two occasions, a child from South Simcoe had won Student of the Year recognition. Schoolyard aggression and violence were a continual problem.

Complaints of disrespect to school staff and local residents were ongoing, and the students were responsible for a high incidence of vandalism and shoplifting in the mall across the street.

But I kept remembering the words of the principal and teachers, and the sudden bright smiles on the faces of the boys and girls I encountered on my visit there. If there are problems, I thought, they certainly don't begin with the children.

I decided to focus on *what I had and what I could do,* instead of what I didn't have and couldn't do. I couldn't change the home conditions or the state of the community around the school, any more than I could change the root causes of many of these problems.

Neither of course could the students. But I could identify the underlying problems preventing students from learning and thriving, and provide a healthy, safe, loving and nurturing environment in which the students could learn, and then teach them what they needed to learn.

When summer vacation arrived, I was making major changes. I remembered how, as a child, I had looked forward to my hours at school. School was a bright, pleasant place to be, among adults who, despite whatever frustrations they may have experienced, really wanted to be there. That summer, I recruited friends and family to add some finishing touches and turn the school into a bright, cheerful and welcoming setting for our students.

One of my friends, Wendy, volunteered to make curtains for the windows. She needed accurate measurements but could only accompany me to the school during evening hours.

The outgoing principal had warned me against visiting the school at night. Not only did we risk returning to our cars to discover the tires slashed or the paint scratched, but incidents of serious violence were not unknown. In fact, as my mother had read in the newspaper, someone was stabbed in the neighboring strip mall the month I assumed my new position at the school.

So we were already a little nervous when we entered the darkened school late one evening. The custodial staff had left hours earlier, and the old building was strangely quiet, with dark corners that threatened to conceal all sorts of perils and menace.

Wendy was standing on a chair holding a measuring tape to

the window, and I was dutifully writing down the dimensions she called out to me, when I distinctly heard footsteps in the darkened hall beyond the room.

"Listen!" I hissed.

We stood frozen to the spot as the footsteps approached, heavy and threatening. Had I locked the front door behind us? I wondered. I was sure I had.

The footsteps stopped, and we heard a door open and close down the hall. Wendy and I looked at each other, holding our breath and trembling a little. The traffic moving outside seemed so remote now. No one would hear us if we screamed.

"We have to see who it is," I whispered.

The footsteps resumed. They were definitely coming closer.

"I can't let you go alone," Wendy said. "I'll come with you." She had been using a hammer to place small nails in the window frame, and now she seized it like a weapon. We both crossed the room and opened the door to the hall, Wendy with the hammer raised and me attempting to hide my fear, with little success. Several feet away, a man confronted us.

"What are you doing here?" I said in my sternest principal voice.

"What am *I* doing here?" he said. "What are *you* doing here?"

I couldn't believe his arrogance. "I am here because I am the principal of this school and I am doing some work," I said in my most authoritative voice. "Now explain who you are."

"I'm the head of security," he said, "and you obviously didn't turn the alarm off when you came in."

All three of us burst into laughter, we were all so relieved. Nevertheless, I received a rather stern lecture on the importance of disarming the security system correctly when entering the building, especially late at night.

I sensed this would not be the last frightening incident I would encounter at South Simcoe School. And, of course, it was not.

My appointment to South Simcoe coincided with the school's seventy-fifth anniversary, and some funds were made available to spruce up the old building in recognition of this milestone. Wendy, the outgoing principal continued to be gracious and welcoming, and we spent a good deal of time talking to staff and visiting other area schools in search of decorating ideas.

Perhaps it's my Indian and Caribbean heritage, but I have always appreciated the ability of color to set a mood. In Trinidad, colors are vibrant and exciting, and it's a joy to wear clothing in rich reds and bright yellows. I felt that the school needed an elegant backdrop for the children's artwork and other displays. Brilliant colors can always be applied here and there in the classroom; the feeling I wanted everyone to experience when first entering South Simcoe was one of welcome and warmth. We narrowed the colors down, then asked the staff to make a final choice. They selected an off-white finish for the walls, with country-blue trim, and the result was perfect.

Among other changes I made was to relocate the principal's office, keeping it on the main floor, the same floor as a grade one classroom. This was, I must confess, partly a practical but also an emotional decision on my part. I wanted to be near loving hugs and smiles provided by "my little darlings," as I called the youngest students, and I wanted to hear them singing together.

There are few greater joys to a teacher than the voices of a grade one class joined in song, lustily and joyfully. I expected to encounter frequent challenges to my normal optimistic state, days when I would feel weighted down with doubts and decisions. On those days, I knew my spirits would be lifted by the sound of young voices singing in a room down the hall, and if I needed an emotional lift, I could always drop in to read stories, or give and receive warm hugs.

In the remaining days and weeks before we welcomed the children on the first day of their new school year at South Simcoe, I continued my focus on creating a warm and welcoming school, which was conducive to learning, and the new paint and bright curtains were just the beginning.

I wanted more than a warm physical environment for learning. I wanted to create an ambience, a climate, that would wrap the staff and the children in positive feelings and make them feel safe and nurtured, as though the school represented the very best place they could be. I wanted the children to be faced with reminders of their value, worth and potential everywhere in the school, and evidence of their successes. Displaying photographs showing them interacting respectfully, performing acts of service and being honored and recognized for their achievements, would model expected behaviors and valued activities.

Posters, stating positive and inspirational thoughts, would focus them on, and remind them that they had within them, the power to make choices that would take their lives in any direction they wished.

I wanted them to anticipate Monday mornings (many children face such disruption in their lives over the weekend, that it leaves them feeling dejected and abandoned), and rejoice in their return to the school after the weekend. I wanted them to feel physically and emotionally safe and secure within its walls, and in years to come be able to look back on their time at South Simcoe and remember it as valuable, fulfilling and memorable.

All of this may make the school sound more like a loving home than a place of learning, but that's the family environment I felt the children needed.

With the principal's office relocated, I moved the kindergarten to a larger room, carpeted the floor and found some money in the budget for new toys and furniture. We added plants and obtained rocking chairs for the teachers to sit in as they read books to the children gathered around to listen.

Does a rocking chair help a teacher read better?

Probably not. Does it add a sense of warmth and security for the children who are listening to the story? Does the type of atmosphere this generates help to "turn students on" to books and reading? Somehow it does, and that's all that counted.

I didn't neglect the staff either; I wanted them to know that they were valued as individuals who needed a place where they could take short breaks during a stressful teaching day, spend quiet time planning and preparing lessons, or simply put their feet up for a minute. The staffroom was relocated out of the basement and onto the main floor. Instead of a dingy refuge, it became a bright and cheerful place for sharing ideas, consultation, celebration and laughter, and it was also more accessible to parents.

Through the balance of the summer, we transformed South Simcoe Public School into "Cinderella prepared for the ball." Over the Labor Day weekend, just hours before the children were to begin their new school year, Ishwar, Shiva, Rishi and I were busy hanging wallpaper in the staff room and adding plants and attractive posters. It was important, I believed, for the renovation to be completed before the students arrived. Students arrive on the first day of school looking their best, and I wanted the school to reflect all the pride and optimism they were feeling.

The involvement of parents, I determined from a very early stage, would be absolutely critical. No matter how attractive the school became and how dedicated the staff were, none of the goals we envisioned could be attained without the support of parents.

We needed them to share our high expectations for our children's success. We needed total co-operation and collaboration—not just periodic attendance at school events, but ongoing involvement in their children's learning; we also wanted to include them in decision-making and problem-solving.

Did this mean that parents who were not well educated themselves, could take an active role in the teaching and learning process? Well, of course!

Even if they hadn't all graduated from secondary school themselves, this did not mean that they couldn't hold these aspirations for their children and support them so that they could finish school and go on to other stages of learning.

I wanted parents and visitors to feel welcome at South Simcoe, so I suggested during a staff meeting that we add a coffee machine in the staff room, and offer parents and visitors a cup of coffee. (At this point in time, this was not the norm.) Someone asked who would pay for the coffee.

"I will," I replied.

Someone else noted that parents might come in just to enjoy a free cup of coffee. I doubted this would always be the case, but if that's what it took to bring parents into the school, I had no problem with the idea. Eventually, at the teachers' request, we installed not only a coffee machine but a large selection of teas and a cooler dispensing spring water.

The small but significant changes continued. At the first staff meeting, we discussed staff attire.

"We are role models in the way we dress and speak and conduct ourselves," I reminded them. The students, I added, needed to see us dressing, speaking and presenting ourselves according to the same standards we expected from them. They agreed unanimously.

With this in mind, we developed a series of agreements that clearly spelled out what this would look like, sound like and feel like.

There was some slight concern when the "looks like" section for attire included an agreement that jeans and track suits would not be worn by teachers and staff during their classroom teaching time. To offset this, we implemented "South Simcoe Days."

These were more casual days, usually on Fridays, when everyone on staff wore South Simcoe Public School T-shirts or sweatshirts. What a beautiful sight it was to see everyone—teachers, principal and custodial staff—all decked out in the school colors, with the school motto and logo emblazoned on the front!

We also agreed that we would all greet the children with a smile and a pleasant "Good morning!" or "Good afternoon!" as they arrived at school. Instead of being seated at our desks, as was the custom, we would be positioned on the stairs, landings and in the hallways, so that the children would be cheerfully greeted and welcomed.

By the time they got to their classrooms, they would have been greeted at least three times by a smiling adult and a friendly word. What a wonderful way for them to begin their school day.

Greeting people cheerfully and politely is a habit that many people grew up with, but it seems to have been lost in recent years. In Trinidad, I remembered being expected to greet everyone with a smile and a friendly word, and this seemed like a worthwhile custom to introduce to South Simcoe.

Another agreement was that our new staff room would be a positive welcoming place, a place where we would plan together, share ideas and feel safe to take intellectual risks without fear of criticism, and where "badmouthing" children, parents, other staff members or any aspect of our activities would be banned. Instead, we would share stories of our students' accomplishments, resources, ideas that worked and generally encourage one another whenever we felt discouraged or overwhelmed.

Changes are rarely made in any system without generating discomfort, and that was the case during one of my meetings with the school staff, early in my first year at the school. When I proposed moving a classroom from the first floor to the second floor, the teacher angrily—and very loudly—objected. "I have been teaching in that classroom for over twenty years," she said. "And now you come in and tell me you're relocating classrooms and putting me upstairs?"

Someone else added, "You seem to think that moving around classrooms and furniture, and adding a fresh coat of paint here and there, is going to solve the problems. Well, they are not. Do you realize the kinds of things we have to deal with here?"

I was taken aback by the anger of these two teachers. Things had been going well to this point. Later, I realized that adjusting to so many changes in such a short period of time can bring feelings of frustration and bitterness to the surface.

"We have students who come to school hungry because there is no food in the house," said the teacher who had objected to having her classroom moved. Her name was Sharon McLean, and I knew she cared about her job and her students with a deep passion. I liked that, even if it meant that I became the target of her frustration and concern.

"Or they'll come to school half asleep because their parents were fighting all night long. Or they'll show up here with cuts and bruises from being beaten. I can understand that you want to create a wonderful environment for our students, and we've all agreed on the idea. But that's not enough. How will paint and new classroom locations solve those problems for our students?"

"They won't," I agreed calmly. "And I'll admit I still have much to learn. But let's think about this. Students who are facing the kinds of challenges our children are, need many things, and one of them is a place where they feel welcome, safe and secure, and where they feel accepted, appreciated, loved and cared for. When they have this, they will be under less emotional stress; therefore, they will be more ready to learn, and we will have a better chance of reaching them.

"Our long-term goal is not only to educate them but also to prepare them to live successfully and take their place in society. In order to do this, we have to help them recognize they have strengths, nurture and develop those strengths, work with them to learn how to deal with triumph and failure, and help them become resilient. We want them to become strong and self-reliant, be prepared to face life's challenges and bounce back. If we can all work together on this goal and uplift our students, perhaps they will have a better future. Isn't this the legacy that we all wish to leave?

"I can't do this alone. It can't be *my* vision; it has to be *our* vision. We all agreed to do what is best for our students and community, and now we need to pull together, support one another and face the challenges together. If we work together in a spirit of harmony, the changes we make will be sustained long after the students have left us and gone on to other stages in their lives. Can we all commit to this? Please tell me we can."

We agreed for the most part. Those who did not, agreed not to sabotage the group effort.

Sharon McLean continued to be my harshest critic, as well as one of my strongest supporters. The same care and concern she had expressed for the students when she raised her voice to me, provided the energy to do what needed to be done, and I will forever thank her for that.

Things were still far from complete on that day in September 1991, when I welcomed the children for the first time as principal. But I could tell from the expressions on their faces that they appreciated the changes that had taken place at South Simcoe.

Their eyes widened at the sight of the bright posters, plants and curtains, and at the teachers who were turned out smartly in jackets, skirts and slacks.

With school underway, I began tackling some housecleaning and decluttering chores. Getting rid of the broken furniture made it easier to function and get our jobs done. To me, keeping the broken and badly mended furniture was like a reminder of past failures.

Many old school buildings, old buildings in fact, tend to be collection points for discarded materials, and the sight of them carried a message that was exactly the opposite of what we wanted to convey. I decided that any broken article that could not be restored to its original condition would be dispensed with. There would be no broken furniture and no makeshift shelving in South Simcoe. These would become reminders of the district's past neglect. (It is very common to withhold spending money on facilities that are slated for closure.)

I wanted to emphasize the future. I was determined to find new ways of accessing resources, and I began to lobby hard with district officials on behalf of the school. After all, I reminded myself, when they sent me to South Simcoe, they knew I would rather store books neatly on a clean floor than have them sitting haphazardly on a broken shelf or table.

When we added newly discarded materials to old furnishings that had been stored in the basement over the years, there was a gigantic pile; in fact, during that first year, we got rid of twelve truckloads of unwanted objects.

Naturally, this "it's good or it's gone" attitude left a few holes in our classroom facilities. But with the clutter gone, we had more room to move about our classrooms and make them more functional and conducive to learning.

Then something occurred that convinced me I was on the right path, and it encouraged my determination to find more ways to make things better for our children.

Several years earlier, while Ishwar and I were living on campus at the University of Western Ontario, I had made friends with a librarian named Lucy Greene. In fact, Lucy hired me to work in the library with her. By the time I arrived at South Simcoe, Lucy was vice-president of Sun Life, a giant insurance firm in Toronto, and she was among the first people I called in search of furnishings.

I couldn't believe my luck. Lucy's job and mine fitted

together like two pieces of a jigsaw puzzle. It was customary at the time for each newly appointed vice-president at her company to order new furnishings for his or her office. It's a corporate status thing, I suppose. In any case, perfectly good desks, chairs, sofas and computer tables—some only a few years or even a few months old—were continuously being replaced by new furnishings to match the new executive's personal taste. Company policy prevented the old furniture from being distributed among its employees, so it sat in limbo, waiting for someone who could use it.

With Lucy's help and her company's generosity, South Simcoe Public School inherited oak credenzas, cozy sofas, comfortable armchairs and a variety of other fine furniture, a far cry from what we moved out. Desks and tables were replaced, and we added sofas to our staff room, the library and to a special parents' meeting room that we created. Many of the children (and some of the teachers, we jokingly said) had never curled up in a chair or worked at a desk as comfortable and attractive as the ones they encountered inside the walls of South Simcoe Public School.

Did I call it luck? I believe it was much more than that.

The exterior of the school was more challenging. On Monday mornings, we often arrived to discover broken beer bottles on the ground, and fresh graffiti on the walls. I have never accepted the idea that these things "just happen" to inner-city schools, and I involved our older students in coming up with ideas to solve this problem.

Talking with them, I learned that the supposed "cure" can sometimes make things worse. That was the case, in part, with South Simcoe. In an effort to avoid vandalism, the school sported no lights on its playground at night. The open area continued to attract older children who had no other place to "hang out," but there was no outlet for their energies, and the prevailing darkness just seemed to encourage silly pranks.

Following the suggestions of our students, we installed lights that turned on whenever anyone was present in the back playground, and added basketball hoops and nets. The vandalism ceased.

Our local member of the provincial legislature was so impressed by this single idea, that he made a point of stopping by the school and commending us on this gesture of generosity to the youth in our community.

At this point, we made one of those decisions that seemed rather small at the time but proved to be significant in the message it carried. When we asked for basketball equipment, someone at the board office offered hoops and backboards that could be removed and stored inside the school building at the end of each day, to thwart vandalism.

We were grateful for their offer, and we knew they meant well, but we politely refused. The message would be precisely opposite to the one I wanted conveyed to the students and the community. I didn't want anything on or in the school that suggested we didn't trust the neighborhood youth, or that we didn't want them on the school grounds.

To children who simply wanted to burn off energy, this would have been a slap in the face. So we insisted on installing hoops and nets that remained in place for anyone who wanted to use them.

It worked! Over time, the broken bottles and graffiti decreased, and one morning we arrived to discover the basketball court festooned with a hundred colorful balloons.

"It's a thank-you note," Sharon said, and I agreed with her totally.

I launched a series of informal chats with senior students at the school, to involve them as young leaders in the changes being made, and to enlist their help in accomplishing them. Everyone was welcome, even those who might not fit the traditional leadership definition, like Ryan.

During one of these chats, I casually suggested that the school needed a mascot, an expression of our pride and identity. They loved the idea, and promised to put their heads together, get input from other students and select one. I assumed they would choose something warm and friendly to reflect the peaceful nature we were trying to create at South Simcoe. You can imagine my horror when the students suggested...a shark!

Sharks are mean, cold-blooded predators, I reminded them. They attack and eat people. Who could ever want something as vicious as a shark for a mascot?

"That's the whole idea," one of the students told me. "We want a mean mascot for sports, so that he can scare the other team. But he can be a friendly mascot to us," said Ryan, one of our more shy students. Then he pulled out a pencil and began drawing, with surprising talent, a whole family of friendly sharks, some smiling and winking, and others doing school work.

I was impressed by his talent and thought process. We would never have thought that Ryan would speak up like this, far less take charge. Empowering the students to choose the mascot, unleashed in students like Ryan a level of leadership, creativity and innovative thinking that might not have emerged in the course of regular classroom activities. How often do children like Ryan get passed over when choosing student leaders?

Once the shark mascot was agreed upon, one of the teachers, Kim Hutchinson, drafted her mother-in-law, Pauline, to depict it throughout the school. We had hired Kim directly out of teachers' college; in addition to being an outstanding teacher, Kim added to the school's success through the sheer power of her enthusiasm.

Pauline is a gifted artist and, within weeks, the lower floor of the school had sharks everywhere. In time, every classroom in the school displayed our shark mascot, our logo, motto and goals.

A shark stood with poised pencil and steno pad on the walls of the school office, and a bespectacled shark, painted on the wall of our library, read a book among shark-infested banners that invited students to "come take a bite out of a book!" Sharks peeked around corners in the downstairs hall, and we even had a shark in the custodian's room—holding a dustpan, of course.

The children were delighted! For some reason, kids are fascinated by fearsome creatures like sharks and dinosaurs. Our sharks were as friendly as you would ever want (or *not* want!) to meet, and their presence elevated the level of pride everyone felt in South Simcoe Public School. I later learned that sharks are not predators of people but that they are survivors—an interesting choice, don't you think?

Somewhere along the way, the staff began referring to me as "Mother Bird." I suppose it was in response to the way I kept talking about nurturing our students until they were prepared to fly off to bigger and better things. "If I'm the Mother Bird," I said jokingly one day, "then South Simcoe is my nest now." The idea of me watching over my "fledglings" was taken one step further, when someone contributed a bottle of gummy worms to my office, and the staff began stopping by to nibble them like a flock of hungry baby birds.

The "Mother Bird" nickname launched Pauline on a new round of mural painting. She found some corners of the school that did not sport a shark, and there she displayed nests of baby birds and a mother arriving to feed them. A little room off the library was painted to depict a Victorian English country garden, with blooming flowers and vines climbing up an elaborate trellis. Joan, our librarian, added lace curtains to the window opening, and placed large, comfy cushions on the floor against the wall. It became "The South Simcoe Secret Garden." We knew the young children would want to curl up there and read books, and they did. But they soon were joined by older children as well, who were drawn to the beauty of this little corner that had sat dark, empty and unused for so many years.

The shark proved to be a great mascot for the students and their sports teams, but we needed something more. We needed a motto with an accompanying symbol to represent our hopes and aspirations for our students, something that would show how we would work together, and something we could use on all official school materials and documents.

We brainstormed—students, staff, parents and community members—and soon, we had a motto: *Together We Light the Way.* It summed up our partnership, students, parents, school and community, working together to light the path of learning.

Next, a symbol to express it visually: We began with "the lamp of learning," the symbol for our school district. Lamps provide light, and light the way through darkness. Then we added hands encircling the lamp to symbolize all of us reaching up, working together.

The motto was great, and everyone loved it, but our symbol needed an artist's touch. One of our students, Sara, told us about her father's skill as a graphic artist. She said he could help us, so I invited him in to meet with us and discuss making our school symbol more pleasing to the eye. He listened attentively to our ideas, promised to create the design, and left. Weeks passed, and we saw nothing more of him, nor of the design. When we asked Sara about her father and his promise, her response was, unfortunately, not surprising.

"Dad's been drinking again," she said, disappointed. "But I'll see if I can get him back here."

She must have been persuasive, because her father showed up again, promised to create the design again...and vanished again. This went on for a few weeks, until I realized that some drastic action was needed if South Simcoe was to have its own school symbol before I retired.

The next time he arrived, at his daughter's request, I poured him a cup of coffee, closed the door to my office, handed him a pencil, several sheets of paper and some colored markers, and said, half-jokingly, that I couldn't let him leave until he finished his assignment. It worked!

This man was truly a gifted artist. He produced a wonderful symbol for us in purple and yellow, the school colors. We especially liked the way the two hands encircled the lamp of learning, in a gesture that suggested protecting our students as they were learning, growing and developing.

Keeping a school clean and tidy is always a challenge, and in spite of the transformation that was taking place, it remained a concern at South Simcoe. In a meeting I held with Gail and Randy, our custodians, Gail explained that she was allotted only half an hour to clean each classroom. Most of the time, she informed me, was spent on removing pencils, pieces of erasers, crumpled papers and other discarded materials from the floor, where they had been tossed by students. "That doesn't leave me much time for dusting and cleaning," she said.

I asked if she had any suggestions for solving the problem. Gail noted that while we were emphasizing teamwork and respectful behavior in the school, it wasn't applied to helping the custodial staff—and she was right. "If we could speak to the students and help them to see things from our point of view, maybe they would understand how they are making things difficult for us," she said.

I thought this was a fine idea and, in consultation with the student leadership team, invited Gail to explain things to one of the senior classes. It made sense that the students should assume some responsibility for their school's cleanliness.

The next day in the classroom, Gail arrived to explain the problem to the students. She entered with a vacuum cleaner, and I watched open-mouthed as she dramatically emptied its contents onto the floor in front of the students. "This is what I picked up from your room yesterday," she told them. She could have picked up even more, she explained, but some items kept clogging her vacuum. "I can't clean your classroom as well as I would like to, because I spend so much of my time picking things off the floor, things that you could be putting in the wastebasket or storing away in your cupboards and desks. If you did your share, I could do a much better job, which would be great teamwork as well as showing me some respect!"

The children were aghast. They had had no idea of the extra work they were creating for Gail; no one had ever explained things to them this way. They immediately began apologizing for the extra work they were creating for an already overworked woman, and began putting their heads together to find a solution.

"How about a fifteen-minute cleanup session at the end of every day?" one student suggested, and the others agreed. Over that term, they influenced all the other students in the school to adopt the idea.

They solved the problem and demonstrated their leadership. This improved things for the whole school. The students showed all of us what they were capable of, if given the opportunity.

And it didn't stop there. A week later, the two custodians came up with a method of recognizing the students' efforts in the school. Each Friday, Gail and Randy selected the cleanest classroom for that week, and presented the class with the Golden Dustpan Award to be displayed proudly. The custodians purchased a dustpan, covered it with gold paint and added a drawing of our shark mascot to it. Every classroom in the school vied to win it at least once during the school year. As a result, we not only had a cleaner school and a stronger team, but two smiling custodians as well.

We also, I hasten to add, had a smarter principal, who realized she could learn a great deal by listening carefully to students and staff, and inviting them to participate in the leadership process.

One day, I received a telephone call from a warm and gracious man named Carl Rimar. Carl, a member of the local Kiwanis Club, had heard of our accomplishments from a social worker and believed in the things we were doing. "You're on the right track," he assured us, and asked how he and other members of his club could partner with us to help.

I suggested that Carl could read to our younger students and chat with the older ones on Monday afternoons, and he did so with such enthusiasm that the students quickly warmed to him. In fact, Mondays became Carl Rimar days at the school. Carl's warm grandfatherly presence enthralled the younger students when reading stories aloud in his mellow voice. Older students grew to trust Carl as an " Uncle," a man to whom they could vent their frustration and always receive a sympathetic ear.

I began referring to Carl as my guardian angel, because he arrived just when we needed someone like him—an understanding and compassionate man who said, simply, "I want to help you." Over time, Carl became a sounding board for new ideas and initiatives; he would always give us a great community perspective. We valued his wisdom and opinions, especially because he always kept in mind our critical decision-making question, *"What's best for our students?"*

Carl submitted ideas of his own, and when he proposed holding a weekend bicycle rodeo for the students, we agreed it was a good one. He suggested holding the rodeo at the school. We would start early on a Saturday morning, and the students would learn the importance of wearing a safety helmet (not law at the time), how to check their bikes for safety and how to negotiate an obstacle course. As icing on the cake, Carl's Kiwanis Club would donate a brand new bicycle to be won in a raffle.

I loved the idea, but I had to agree with some of Sharon McLean's concerns. Friday night was "party night" in the South Simcoe area, and many of the students might have difficulty arriving for an early start on Saturday morning—not to mention the adult volunteers. We had never held an event like this at the school, which made the response of the students and their parents unpredictable. What if no one showed up? What if it rained? What if…?

We ran the gamut of what-ifs and decided to hold the First Annual South Simcoe Bike Rodeo in spite of so many misgivings. Even if just twenty people showed up early on Saturday morning, I pointed out, we would consider the event a success; so let's do it. With Sharon's realistic cautions in mind, we went ahead organizing the event, and I went home on Friday evening looking forward to it.

When I woke up early the next morning and looked out my bedroom window, I saw…rain. Steady, depressing, drizzly rain falling from a low grey sky. As I dressed and prepared to drive to the school, I refused to accept the possibility of being defeated by bad weather, and I began willing the rain away.

The rain was still falling when I arrived at the school about eight o'clock and found a series of puddles and a half-dozen soggy community partners waiting for me. "I'm willing the sun to arrive!" I announced, which generated some uncertain smiles from Carl and the others.

Things got better almost immediately. The rain became a light mist and soon ceased completely. The small group grew steadily with the improving weather until, by ten-thirty, about a hundred students, Kiwanis Club members and parent volunteers were on hand.

Soon the sun was shining in all its warmth, the puddles were vanishing, the students were learning important safety rules and the Kiwanis members were fulfilling their mandate of providing service to their community.

Had we brought the sun to South Simcoe with the sheer force of our will and determination that nothing would spoil the day for our students? Doubt it if you will, but I remain convinced anyway.

Lessons for all of us were learned in various ways at South Simcoe. When I learned, from Pat Coles, a parent whose mother had attended the school, that South Simcoe had once boasted lovely rose gardens along the south wall, we decided to restore the grounds to their original splendor. That spring, Jacki Devolin, one of our teaching assistants, recruited a team of students to canvass the neighborhood for volunteers, old gardening tools and bedding plants. Many of the people they approached were pleasantly surprised to learn we were not looking for money. We didn't want their money—we wanted their support and involvement as community members. Anyway, their contributions would beautify the school as well as the community, since the gardens would bloom all summer long.

We had another, more subtle motive behind our gardening efforts. We wanted to demonstrate how many things of little or no value to others—including used and often broken garden tools, rejected spindly plants and even the long-ignored grounds surrounding the school—could be put to good use with a little love, care, time and effort.

Sharon, bless her heart, came up with the idea of planting flowers in front of the nearby Legion Hall as well, as a "thank you," for partnering with us and allowing us to use their facilities.

We organized our first Community Celebration Day, and not even the rain that day could dampen the enthusiasm of our planting team. Included on the team were Ruth, our school trustee, local business people, community service club members and a large team of staff and students.

At Ruth's suggestion, we all cut armholes in plastic garbage bags, slid them on as waterproof vests, tied others around our heads as hats and set to work. Once again, we discovered we had set something in motion that was much larger than anticipated.

We all took turns watering the flowers during the summer, but more than our periodic efforts were necessary to keep the flowers blooming. Two employees of the Kmart store, in the plaza across the street, began to have lunch beneath the trees in our garden. When they noticed the flowers were wilting from the heat, they borrowed a sprinkling can from the store's garden display and watered them thoroughly.

Our second Community Celebration Day expanded to include a fun fair on the playground, complete with ponies carrying delighted students on their backs; they were led around the grounds by two staff members. Inside the school, invited guests munched on cookies and sandwiches, and were entertained by songs and presentations from each class.

From there, Community Celebration Day seemed to acquire a life of its own. In the following years, members of our planting team included the mayor, various politicians, school board officials, mascots from all the local businesses, several police officers, firefighters, and so many other partners, that we were running short of room to plant the flowers. Our grade eight students, who were on their way to high school, tended the gardens during the summer vacation.

Community Celebration Day activities grew to include the community touring the school and visiting classrooms. We wanted our community partners to see for themselves the difference their assistance was making to the students and their education. The students, of course, relished the opportunity to show off their achievements—a win-win situation.

In every classroom, students placed their *Together We Light the Way* portfolios on their desks, prepared to demonstrate and discuss their accomplishments one-on-one with their visitors. These accomplishments were wide-ranging and invariably impressive to the community partners—not just because of the way the students described the good choices they had made and the goals they had achieved, but because of the way they supported their stories with evidence, with data and graphs, to demonstrate their progress in reading, writing, mathematics, behavior, teamwork and leadership.

In later years, as our programs spread to other schools and communities, electronic portfolios replaced the paper ones, and the presentations became even more impressive.

We learned several lessons from Community Celebration Day. We discovered that everyone wants to see students succeed and be a part of that success; we also learned how powerful a school and community can be when they work together to help students learn and succeed. Soon, there was no need to reach out for assistance—we often were offered more than we could use.

Community Celebration Day also taught a lesson to the small handful of skeptics. "The school planted flowers there before," they said when we first proposed the idea, "and vandals always ripped them out."

None of the flowers from Community Day were ever "ripped out." Why? Because "the school" hadn't planted them. They had been planted by the entire community, including the students, the staff and the mayor, plus police officers, firefighters, business people, mascots and service club members. So many people could say, "This is our garden."

Other lessons were learned from the garden as well, including some we neither wanted nor anticipated.

When an overenthusiastic student knocked off a branch from one of the young trees planted on our grounds one day, he used it as a weapon, chasing others across the play area. They in turn ripped more branches from the tree to fight back, and before Cathie, one of the supervising teachers, could bring a halt to the mayhem, ten branches had been torn from the little tree.

Cathie carried them in her arms to my office, her eyes welling up. "Look what they did, Sandra," she said. "Look what our students did. I can't believe it after all the time we have spent teaching them to respect the environment."

"No." I couldn't believe it. "Not our students?" I said.

"Yes," she said, "*our* students."

"Tell me they're all new to our school," I almost pleaded. South Simcoe students didn't go around destroying property. They respected their school and the environment, and this kind of thing went against everything we were striving to teach them. These must have been new students who hadn't yet tuned in to our way of doing things.

"They're not new," she said. "They just got carried away."

I rarely became angry, but this one struck a nerve. "I need to see them all," I said to Cathie. It meant removing students from class, something I rarely did, but it was an expression of how seriously we took such a breach of our agreement to respect the environment. I was also disappointed and frustrated.

With all the students gathered in my office, looking sheepish and, I admit, a little anxious, I displayed the branches to them. "How could this happen?" I asked. "How could our students, students of this school, do such a thing? How could children such as you, who take pride in our school and in our gardens, do such damage to this poor little tree? Please tell me there is some explanation for this."

They blurted out a series of explanations. "We were just fooling around." "We got carried away." "We didn't mean to."

I could see they were truly sorry, but I also saw an opportunity to teach an important lesson, and I didn't want this to ever happen again. Students, I knew, could appear to be destructive when they were simply being thoughtless.

"Do you realize you severely injured a living thing?" I asked them. They hadn't considered things in that light before. "A tree has life," I said. "A different kind of life from your own, but it's still a life." I held up the branches for them to see. "This is what you did to a living thing." Then I set the branches on a table in my office and sat staring at them, as though I were mourning them, while the children found their way back to their classes.

The next day, I carried the branches in my arms from class to class and explained what had happened to them. I didn't name the students responsible for the damage, because I didn't want revenge or punishment; I wanted everyone to understand the seriousness of the matter.

I explained how sad it made me and the other teachers, how the torn and damaged branches demonstrated a complete lack of respect for a living thing and for the environment, and how this behavior was certainly not what we had all agreed to from our wonderful students. Then I asked for suggestions to ensure this never ever happened again.

The students took things seriously. Suggestions were made, and some even proposed that anyone who went closer than ten feet to a tree should be suspended. We did not go that far, of course. The point had been made, the lesson learned. The offending students offered to make amends by working in the garden and restoring the area around the tree. Interestingly, they continued to do this well beyond the expected time and told their friends that they really enjoyed gardening.

Our care for the garden in many ways reflected our care for the students who attended the school, and the garden was so beautiful that South Simcoe Public School won the "Looking Good Award," as the most attractive of over 100 elementary schools in the district.

Changes to the school's inner and outer appearance made an impact, no doubt. But the major challenge lay ahead. We had to help our students make personal changes, develop a belief in themselves and their capabilities, envision a brighter future for themselves, and succeed academically. This involved so much more than appearance; it involved touching their hearts as well as their minds, and even deeper.

Does your problem solving model/method
address root cause or band aid solutions?
If you would like to find out about my proven steps
to creating root cause solutions to problems,
please go to my website: APublicSchoolMiracle.com.

Chapter 4

Confronting the Bully

As we grew up, many of us were taught that to love and be loved is one of life's greatest gifts. But nothing prepares you for the hole left in your heart when you lose someone you love. The unexpected loss I suffered during that first year at South Simcoe was no less painful and searing just because I was learning to love the students, staff and community of South Simcoe School. In some ways, this made it more agonizing.

I had come to South Simcoe Public School with many hopes and expectations, but with very few answers. In fact, I learned that there is never a single answer or set of answers when dealing with the challenges facing students in areas such as South Simcoe. We had to create our own solutions by all working together on our common goal.

During September of my first year at South Simcoe, two grade eight boys raced down the hall towards my office, followed by several other worried students. I heard them coming, shouting as they ran, "Where's the principal? Where's the principal?"

"What's the problem?" I asked. "What is going on?"

"A man in a truck tried to take away two of our girls!" they said.

The abduction of a student is a nightmarish fear faced by teachers and parents alike. I asked where the girls were, trying to conceal my apprehension.

"We have them," one boy said, and the other added, "They're only six years old."

The girls had been walking home through the mall, opposite the school, when a man drove up in a van and offered them some candy. When they approached to take it from his hand, he tried to pull them inside. The two grade eight boys, witnessing the attempted abduction, rushed to the vehicle and pulled the girls away. The boys also alertly recorded the van's license number, proving that despite—or because of—the challenges confronting many students at South Simcoe, they were very streetwise.

Two detectives arrived in response to my telephone call and interviewed me, the grade eight boys and the little girls who had almost been abducted. When they completed the interviews and began to leave, one of the girls tugged at my skirt. "Ask for their badge numbers," she said, indicating the officers.

I was a little confused, and asked why it was important.

"In case you need more information," she replied.

Even the detectives were impressed. "She's right," one of them said. "You need both an incident number and a badge number. That way, when you need information about the progress of the case, we can quickly find the information and bring you up to date on our progress."

After the police left, I looked down at this little waiflike beauty who, just an hour or so before, had narrowly missed being abducted in broad daylight by a sexual predator.

"Are you all right?" I asked.

She smiled as though to reassure me, the adult and professional educator. "Yes, I'm fine," she said. Then she asked if I was all right, and advised me not to worry. With the excitement behind her, and confident that I had survived the event as well as she had, she skipped down the hall as though she didn't have a worry in the world.

Me? I remained frazzled for the rest of the day.

We were continually being surprised by the street-smart character and maturity of the students at South Simcoe. One day, a member of our staff, a bright young teacher named Doug Beeston, was reading to a kindergarten class. They remained quiet and attentive until Doug came to a passage in the book that referred to babies springing from cabbage patches. Suddenly the entire class shot their hands up in the air. "That's not where they come from!" the students protested, and before Doug could respond, one boy began reciting the process of procreation in exquisite and colorful detail, while all the other children nodded soberly in agreement.

The children were calm about the event, but Doug was still

flustered when he described the incident to me later that day. "I just wanted to read them a story," he said. "I didn't want to teach a sex education class to a bunch of five-year-olds." I assured him we all had much to learn from our street-wise student body.

Other events faced by the staff were not quite as humorous, and often more dramatic. One day early in September, I called in a supply teacher for a teacher who was ill. Unfortunately, this was a class in which several children had serious mental health issues, and the supply teacher had no real experience with this type of situation. The students' behavior was very challenging and, halfway through her teaching day, the supply teacher threw up her hands and told me that she was leaving; she had had enough, and she fled the school.

This left me with no one except Andrea, a fairly new teacher, to supervise the class. Andrea said there was total pandemonium in the classroom. This was in sharp contrast to other classrooms where students were working and moving about quietly and respectfully. Andrea discovered one of the students, an extremely bright girl, barking like a dog. The girl had removed her shoes and stockings, and had placed wads of tissues between her toes to look like a dog's paw.

While this was happening, another student was performing somersaults across the desks, risking broken bones or worse, and a third announced that Andrea was not to speak directly to her but to her stuffed toy mouse.

Andrea was able to deal with the situation by refocusing the students on their Classroom Behavioral Agreements, and using tried and true school-wide strategies we had put in place and all agreed to use. The students soon fell into their familiar routine.

Andrea knew, from information in the teacher's planning book, that the girl who was barking like a dog suffered from a multiple personality disorder, and was awaiting placement in a high-care facility. The student who insisted on the teacher talking not to her but to her "pet mouse," was experiencing serious psychological trauma.

The one doing somersaults was simply angry and needed a "safe place" to cool down. (A safe place was an agreed-upon location, such as my office or the library, where students could go when they needed to calm down, and stay until they felt ready to rejoin the class). Andrea remained calm and confident and saved the day.

Often, it seemed as though each time we solved a problem or overcame an obstacle, another appeared to take its place. How could we possibly keep up with this volume of new (and sometimes reappearing) challenges? The answer was teamwork, a conscious and consistent way of dealing with behavior, and a special staff, of course.

Our staff meetings were largely to gather as a whole staff to share ideas and experiences, discuss issues of concern and learn from one another.

.Together, we were able to identify strategies that helped the students, and then work on those strategies, refine them and then use them consistently throughout the school.

Instead of one long monthly meeting, we met for a short time every two weeks.

In order to honor and respect everyone's commitments beyond the school day, we never went over time.

How did we manage to fit in so many concerns, and enable so many people to express their views in this short time? In a word: organization. We all worked to make the meetings informative and fun, even while we were working hard to develop solutions, discuss issues and share ideas.

For example, every session began with music, and snacks to enjoy. More important, we insisted on focusing on positive results. We kept asking, "What worked well?" and "What can we do to make it even more effective?" Everyone knew that their opinion was valued and their ideas would be given serious consideration. This did more than generate effective ideas—it also gave everyone a true sense of partnership in the running of the school. We became a large, inclusive and cohesive team, sharing leadership, and we were all committed to achieving our goal of making a positive difference in the lives of our students.

During my first year at South Simcoe, it quickly became apparent that the most immediate goal academically was teaching our students to read. When I had taught grade one, my goal had been to have my students reading by the end of the school year. Yet during that first year at South Simcoe, we had large numbers of students unable to read in grade five.

This was a reflection of the reality of the South Simcoe community, the transient nature of many families there and the social and economic difficulties faced by both the parents and students. When students are being distracted by major problems at home—problems ranging from hunger to severe physical and mental abuse—the intense concentration required for learning simply vanishes.

Working with trustee Ruth Lafarga as our champion, we started small and set a realistic goal of every South Simcoe student reading by grade five. We knew that achievement of this goal was impossible without the wholehearted support and assistance of our parents.

To involve them, Goal-Achievement books were developed and sent home with every student, in the "Wednesday Envelope." Parents were informed of goals that were set and progress made by the end of every day, strategies that were working well and suggestions as to how they could assist. It was like having a customized weekly report card. Students needing higher levels of support took their books home daily.

This system taught the students that we cared about their parents' opinions, and that their parents cared about what we were saying, that we both held the same high expectations for them, and we were working together to help them to succeed. This also prevented surprises at report card time.

Using the system effectively, and integrating it into all

classrooms, took some time. We began by introducing it in one class, working through implementation issues and refining the system. Then we added three more classes in the second year and, by the third year, it was being used throughout the school.

I might have tried to move faster, had it not been for Sharon who cautioned me, "This system is excellent, but it takes time to learn how to use it properly; please go slowly, and give everyone time to catch their breath."

We had honest and open dialogues about implementation difficulties and how we could refine the system in a way that would benefit everyone, not just those who could adapt to change quickly. In many ways, these difficulties and their resolutions actually strengthened us as a team.

Inevitably, regrettable incidents occurred. Once, I suggested to a veteran male teacher that some simple adjustments to his report cards might make them easier for the parents of his students to understand. We had all agreed on two things about report cards: one, that they would be written in simple language, easy for parents to understand; and two, that the opening comment on every report card would be a positive one about the child. After all, we were writing to a parent about their child.

He had never in all his 28 years of teaching had anyone ask him to adjust his report cards—certainly not a brand new principal—and he responded by throwing the report cards on my desk and swearing at me, in front of a group of parents and students who happened to be passing in the main hallway. I put on a brave face, but I admit I drove home in tears; I hate being yelled at, and I certainly was not used to anyone swearing at me.

Later, we came to an agreement; he agreed to redo his report cards, and I gave him some extra time to do this. We shook hands, vowing to make every effort to work together to make a positive difference for our students. I learned I could be yelled at and survive, that timing was critical and, most of all, that flexibility is a part of every successful negotiation.

Many things were falling into place, and progress was being made. Our goals, which some once said were overly ambitious and unattainable, were now being achieved. Christmas was coming, and we were all looking forward to another term of student success, the joy of the holiday season and, of course, a much-needed break from routine.

Then, on the very afternoon that I was handed the rewritten report cards, my brother called to inform me that my father had died. The words came to me through a blur of emotion and gloom: a heart attack; no warning; sixty-six years old; much too young.

The death of a parent is traumatic for everyone, and I do not intend to suggest that I suffered any more pain or sadness than anyone else in my situation. But everything seemed so unfair. Here I was, determined to improve the lives of our students, creating a team of wonderfully dedicated professionals, demonstrating all the beliefs I had held throughout so much of my life and teaching career…and I had been so busy that I couldn't remember the last time I had told my father I loved him. What did all my achievements mean now?

They meant as much as ever, of course. I knew that in my heart. But as the eldest child in our family, I had enjoyed a special relationship with my father. When I was a small child, he would rock me gently on his knee and read to me from storybooks. He taught me how to draw flowers, and he had a special way of whistling my name when he arrived home from work. He told me I was the most special girl in the world and that I could achieve anything I wanted to as long as I remembered who I was, believed in myself and remained strong inside. He always said, " I believe in you and will always believe in you, no matter what!" Naturally, I believed him, and that belief has kept me strong over the years and helped me through all the tough times. It is at the core of who and what I am today.

I know that millions of parents express the same kind of love and support to their children each day, and their children are blessed because of it. But this was my father saying these things to me, and despite what my mind knew, my heart had always believed he would live forever. Now he was gone, without even a goodbye spoken between us. He was the first close relative I had lost to death, and to say I was devastated as I replaced the receiver after that telephone call...well, there are no words to describe my emotions.

With guidance from officials at the board office, arrangements were made for me to be away from the school.

Then I set off for my sad journey to Trinidad.

The days I spent there are now a jumble of memories—tears, hugs, stories of my father's kindnesses, and a reaffirmation of all that my family meant to me. I returned to Canada during the Christmas vacation, with a strange longing simply to stay at home. As much as I loved the students and the challenge I had accepted at South Simcoe, I was emotionally drained and unable to find the energy to continue dealing with the stress and struggle involved in realizing our vision for the school.

Let's face it, I discovered myself thinking one day, you are an inexperienced principal dealing with some very experienced staff members, and you are trying to make a lot of changes without alienating those around you. You may believe in what you are doing, but until everyone around you believes it, shares the same vision with the same passion and commits to undertaking the journey, you aren't going to achieve your goals. Accept that making the changes you envision will be a long, slow and often painful process.

I was ready to listen.

Some obstacles at the school that seemed overwhelming had nothing to do with the students and staff. In spite of assistance from surprising sources, such as Lucy at Sun Life, the school still needed essential items like good bulletin boards and classroom equipment. The delays in obtaining furnishings and materials, and the tight restrictions on expenditures, were doubly frustrating because we were starting to see what we could accomplish with the right resources.

I knew that other school principals were facing the same challenge of limited funds and equipment, but it seemed doubly unfair to us at South Simcoe. In my emotional state, I seriously questioned whether I could maintain the confidence I had shown to others—a confidence I felt eroding within me after my father died. I simply did not want to return to South Simcoe. I wanted only to stay at home, where I felt safe and warm and loved.

That's when another of those events that others call "luck" occurred. I prefer to think of it as proof of the Eastern proverb: When the student is ready, the teacher appears.

About a week before school resumed, at the very height of my self-doubts, I was introduced via telephone to Steven Ramsanker. Steven had just been awarded the Order of Canada for his work at the Alex Taylor Community School in Edmonton, a school that had been facing many of the same challenges as South Simcoe. Like me, Steve was from Trinidad, which made it easy for me to talk with him by telephone.

As I spoke to Steve, I felt my doubts begin to fade and my resolve return. Part of it was the familiar island lilt in his voice, and part of it was his enormous energy and infectious sense of humor. "I'm a Rhodes scholar," he would say to people when meeting them for the first time. Then giving them a sly look, he would add, "The railroads." After immigrating to Canada, Steve had paid for his college education by working on the railway in

Western Canada. It was Steve's description of his experiences at Alex Taylor Community School, however, that I most wanted to hear. The school was in Edmonton's toughest neighborhood, set among taverns and cut-rate hotels, where students had to thread their way among prostitutes and drug dealers on their way to and from classes. The annual murder rate in the compact Alex Taylor neighborhood often equaled the rate in all the neighborhoods in the rest of the city combined.

Steve's educational philosophy was remarkably similar to mine, and he had a great deal more experience. To alleviate the hunger of students who often arrived at school without breakfast, Steve served them early-morning meals of moose-meat cakes and fried bannock, as well as more traditional fare, often paid for out of his own pocket.

Food wasn't the only need faced by these students. Many wore tattered, dirty clothing because they had no washing facilities, so Steve actually convinced the school district to install showers, a washing machine and a clothes dryer in the school for students to use to keep themselves clean and tidy. This made a huge difference to his students. In addition to having food and being clean, they also felt better about themselves and began to improve academically as well.

Steve's dedication to his work and his students was nothing less than awe-inspiring. He wanted the students at Alex Taylor to realize that another world existed beyond their inner-city neighborhood. On three occasions, he took students to his native Trinidad to experience the culture and values there—once mortgaging his house to cover the expenses. During his stint at Alex Taylor, he had arranged for over 2,500 students and 400 seniors to travel across Canada and the United States and into the Caribbean. As word of his achievements spread, Steve was often tempted away from Alex Taylor by offers from government and university groups, but he loved what he was doing and stubbornly chose to remain where he was. "This is my purpose in life; this is what I was born to do, and I am happy here," he would say, sounding very much like my grandmother.

When I expressed the misgivings I had been feeling, Steve's response was, "The path you have chosen is not an easy one. You have chosen to tackle the root cause of your students' problems; this is really hard work. You will have to draw on all the strength you have inside, and reach beyond yourself to give your students what they need." I must have expressed at least a little doubt, because he added, "You can do it. You will do it. I'll be here to support you. Call me anytime you need me."

Steve's inspiring words were like a tonic to me. I resolved to continue pursuing our goals at South Simcoe, discarding any idea of giving up in favor of reading in a cozy chair at home every day. Steve entered my life at the right time, with the messages I needed to hear. He was like a lifeline to me at the time.

I returned to the school after the death of my father, a changed person in many ways. Students, staff and parents were extremely supportive, reaching out to help and comfort me in any way they could. Even those who did not support my changes, supported me as a person in my time of loss. They tell me that I became more patient, a better listener and more willing to accept that change would take more time. On reflection, I think the passing of my father strengthened his lessons of tolerance and care for others in me; it helped me to gain a deeper appreciation of the people around me, and it helped me to mature as a human being.

Inspiring and strengthening our team became even more important. I encouraged, I participated and I learned to accept, include and listen carefully, even to those who resisted change. I knew now that I could not change all that needed changing by myself, like some warrior riding alone to do battle with injustice. That was comic-book fantasy.

At South Simcoe, we dealt with real-life challenges every day, challenges that demanded the skills, expertise and passion of a strong, dedicated and committed team.

The benefits were beyond measure.

An example of a real-life challenge came with the arrival of Desmond Harris, an angry grade eight student who was continuously bullying younger students, including his own younger brother. We had worked hard to eliminate bullying in the school, and now there were very few incidents of bullying. We were certainly not going to allow Desmond to continue his unacceptable behavior.

We tried a number of strategies, but we knew we needed

co-operation from his parents if we were to be successful at changing his behavior. Our attempts to involve his parents proved fruitless; in their eyes, Desmond was "just being a boy," and they did nothing to support our efforts.

Desmond's problems became a nightmare during a visit by his class to the Royal Ontario Museum in Toronto, where Desmond stole and ate students' lunches and deliberately damaged an exhibit before running off to hide in a washroom. When they were unable to locate him, museum officials cancelled the class tour, disappointing dozens of students. Museum officials also stated, in no uncertain terms, that Desmond would not be welcomed back.

Back at the school, I discovered more. Desmond had bullied several younger students; he took their lunch money, locked them up in an old tool shed in a neighbor's yard, and then taunted them by throwing them pieces of pizza that he had purchased with their money. Desmond's parents gave Desmond a good allowance for his lunch, so it didn't seem that hunger was the issue here. Desmond really seemed to enjoy terrorizing others.

I made the decision to suspend Desmond from school for a few days. I did this with some regret, because I knew that this would not help Desmond to improve his behavior and become more responsible, but the younger students had the right to feel safe at school. Suspensions were always a last resort, never a solution.

The interesting thing about Desmond was that, in spite of his actions, I sensed a goodness within him. That's not the opinion of some idealistic dreamer, by the way. I talked to Desmond and watched him respond to my words. When he was ready to listen and you reasoned with him, for a time, he would become the most wonderful child, before sliding back into his role as an angry, resentful bully.

What I remember most fondly about Desmond was his voice. He sang in the school choir, and frequently took solos. When he did, the sound of his voice could bring tears to your eyes, and suddenly he was no longer a bully but a specially gifted child. I need to make this point because it is too easy to measure a child's progress according to only one or two dimensions.

Yes, Desmond was aggressive and hostile, but he was as complex as any human being; and the special qualities within him justified all the effort we expended on him. Unfortunately, it came to naught, with disturbing consequences for me. Nothing else had motivated Desmond's parents to become actively involved in the school, but our decision to suspend him generated an immediate and hostile reaction.

Desmond's father arrived at my office the following day, furious with me for suspending his son for what he considered a harmless and playful incident. Mr. Harris was a large man who towered over me and my staff, and his very presence was intimidating.

Desmond's very attractive teacher had told me that he

always tried to arrange meetings with her late in the evening, when he knew the custodians had left for the day; she said that he ogled her as if undressing her with his eyes. She had never reported this, because she wasn't sure if it was all in her head, but she quickly filled me in when she heard I was arranging a meeting with him.

Now his anger exploded into screams and threats, all of them directed at me, and my explanations only seemed to fuel his hostility. I had to stand my ground. Staff and students, I knew, were aware of our encounter. They could hear Desmond's father ranting and raving, thumping the desk and shouting abuse at me, acting in the same manner that we had been telling students was unacceptable from them. How then could it be acceptable from this man? I refused to lift the suspension on Desmond, and Mr. Harris finally left my office, spewing threats against me, the school, the school district and much of the universe.

The next morning, Mr. Harris returned. He stormed past my secretary and some children gathered around her, entered my office and slammed the door shut. With his fist raised, he started shouting curses and threats. "I am here to deal with you, you bitch!" he roared, banging his fist on my desk, "I'm going to teach you a lesson that you will never forget."

I sat at my desk, petrified. "I'm fed up with you," he said before I could speak. "I'm sick of you picking on my boy, picking on my family and picking on me!" I managed to remain outwardly calm, but I was scared.

Quickly realizing that I was dealing with a classic bully, I decided to take action. I stood up slowly and deliberately, looking him straight in the eye. He stood between me and the door. "Get out of my way now!" I said in my loudest and most authoritative voice. My no nonsense manner obviously caught him off guard, because he reacted by stepping aside. I quickly walked out of my office into the open, where a small crowd of students and staff had gathered.

"Call the police," I said to Joan when I opened the door. "This man is bullying and threatening me; I want him arrested." Wide-eyed, she reached for the telephone. Students, who had witnessed the man's actions and overheard his angry shouts, watched with concern, and one six-year-old girl burst into tears, running to me and hugging me, asking if I was all right. I assured her I was fine just as the man strode out of my office, subdued a little by my instruction to call the police.

"Don't think this is the end of this," he said, pointing his finger at me. "You just wait!" I found out later that Desmond's father had lost his job a week earlier, and whether this was the cause of his rage, or as a result of his rage, it was unclear. It didn't matter.

His fury grew worse; it was white-hot, all of it aimed at me. He even visited the director of education at her office, sweeping documents from her desk onto the floor in an explosion of rage before leaving. He then contacted the minister of education, but his rude and aggressive behavior got him nowhere.

Unable to find support from official sources, he launched into an even more bitter personal attack on me. Soon, letters began arriving, calling me a bitch, a tyrant, and using other unspeakable words to express his opinion of me. He placed copies of his letters under the windshield wipers of cars in our parking lot, in the mall across the street and in the neighborhood.

The day that happened, I drove home in tears. Once again, I began questioning my decisions, my resolve and my ability to do the job I had to do at South Simcoe. One parent, familiar with Desmond's father and his actions, advised me to back down. "He's a bully," she said. "He won't give you a moment's peace. He terrorizes us in the neighborhood until we give in to him. Why not just drop the whole thing and get on with your life? It's not the end of the world."

Perhaps she was right. I could back down and make the situation go away. After all, I expected hurdles when I accepted the position, but not character assassination or the threat of physical violence. Besides, I didn't suspend Desmond in a moment of spite or frustration. It was a carefully considered decision, made after going through the pages and pages of documented evidence of his bullying and extortion, and after repeated interventions to stop or at least curb his inappropriate behavior. We could not accept Desmond's bullying behavior, and he needed to make an effort to change.

My husband, Ishwar, as always, provided a solid foundation of support. "Do what you know is right in your heart," he advised. "Do what you can live with and what you can talk to our children about without being ashamed or embarrassed. We will support and love you no matter what."

For a very long time, I sat quietly reassessing everything I had done, and all the difficulties it had created. The truth is, I seriously considered backing away from the issue. Was this man justified in his anger at me? Had I done the correct thing after all? Should I back down or continue to stand firm, making things more difficult for everyone at the school and the district office?

I went back and forth with these questions all evening, and one thing was clear. The man was a bully, no more and no less. As a school, we had significantly reduced bullying and were now working on eliminating it and preventing it from recurring. We knew that it was not a simple childhood problem. We understood the long-term harmful effects of bullying. How then could I simply walk away from this bullying situation, just to make life easier for myself? What kind of message would that send to our students? What kind of role model would I be? I finally went to bed, knowing the answer.

A few days later, I invited the teachers to a meeting at my home. This was my personal issue, so it seemed a more appropriate venue. They were already aware of most of the details and knew that I was the cause of all this disruption. I asked for their counsel and welcomed their opinions and ideas.

I told them that I wanted to hold firm and not lift the suspension but that I realized that any decision I made would affect them as well. I explained that if I stood my ground, the bully could extend his threats to them as well, and they might become targets of his abuse. Everyone, bless their hearts, backed me one hundred percent, and assured me that I had their full support.

"We have said that bullying is unacceptable and that's that," stated Sharon. That meeting, and my obvious need for their personal as well as professional support, brought all of us closer, and we became even more dedicated to eradicating bullying. It was the first time I had spoken to them so openly about my personal feelings and fears, and I realized how much like a family we were becoming.

The bullying and harassment continued. Standing firm did not make Mr. Harris go away; in fact, he became more irate. He began to stalk me and wait for me in the parking lot to accost and scream threats at me. Teachers and even parents began escorting me to my car. Since he had ignored my trespass letter, we lodged an official complaint with the police and obtained a court order warning him against trespassing in the school, but with little effect; he ignored that too. This, by the way, is not as unusual as you might think. He continued to lurk about, sometimes on the schoolyard, sometimes boldly entering the building and walking out again just to prove we were unable to banish him. And so it continued, through the balance of the school year.

But something good came of this. Parents began thanking me for taking a stand against him. Many of them began standing up to him as well when he tried to bully them. Their support for me extended into stronger support for the school. By standing up to this bully, I taught a lesson to our students and earned the respect and appreciation of their parents. This, combined with the bonding that resulted from the meeting at my home, made us all a tighter, more cohesive group, prepared to do whatever was necessary to make South Simcoe the kind of school we all wanted it to be. That's the ironic result of this entire episode, as painful and disturbing as it was.

At year's end, when Desmond completed grade eight and went on to high school, his father gave up. A twinge of sadness runs through my memory when I recall this. As I mentioned earlier, at heart, Desmond was a decent kid. We built a stronger team at the school as a result of his father's outrageous actions, it's true. But although there appears to have been no alternative to our actions, I feel we somehow all failed Desmond. And I still miss hearing his sweet voice singing in the choir.

My dreadful experience with Desmond and his father was balanced by several smaller, less dramatic but no less important episodes. All of them taught us things about our students and their needs. Many involved students like Janice, whose need was so basic we almost overlooked it.

Janice was a grade eight student with learning problems. She had failed earlier grades at other schools, leaving her well behind her friends. In spite of great progress made, Janice did not qualify to advance to high school the following year. This news was like a blow to Janice, and she felt that she couldn't handle what she saw as humiliation. Her social worker, who was trying to guide, support and encourage her, told us that Janice was talking about dropping out of school.

"What will I say to people? I want to go to high school with my friends," Janice tearfully confessed to her. "If I can't go to high school, I'll quit school; I'm too old to be hanging around with the students at South Simcoe for another year."

Thanks to the fact that she liked her new teacher and was receiving a great deal of personalized assistance, Janice had made enormous progress over the school year. We knew that if she stayed with us for another year, she could graduate with good marks. None of us wanted to see her toss away her best chance to obtain an education; and even though we understood her frustration and her embarrassment, we knew it was the best choice academically.

Passing her on to high school seemed like writing her off, and we simply couldn't do that—how could we write off one of our students? I invited her to my office for a chat, and I asked Jacki, who was especially fond of Janice, to sit in.

"Is it true you're thinking of dropping out of school?" I asked Janice when we were settled.

She nodded glumly, avoiding my eyes.

"I don't understand why you would think of doing such a

thing," I said. "Especially now, when you are doing so well. We're so proud of your achievements. Aren't you proud of yourself?"

"I guess so," Janice said. She looked so forlorn and confused. Her eyes began to fill with tears. "I just want to be with my friends more than I want to be here."

"Everyone wants to be with friends," I said. "But your education is important too. You have been working so hard, and your teachers have worked hard to help you, Janice. You're so close to graduating with good marks; don't you care about this? I do; we all do—we all care about you and want the best for you."

She looked directly at me for the first time, with an expression of hope and maybe surprise.

"You do? You really care about me?"

"We do, Janice," I assured her. "We care about you. All of us." Then I added, "And we love you, Janice. We care about you and love you. Don't you know that?"

"You never said that before," she said. "You never said that you cared about me or loved me."

"Janice, you know I love you," Jacki said. I had never seen such relief and gratitude in a child's eyes as I saw when Janice heard those words.

"We all do, and we want you to succeed. We want you to stay in this school and get the foundation you need for your future."

"I needed to hear you say that," Janice said. Then she

smiled, her eyes glistening with tears. "OK," she said. "I'll stay, and if anyone teases me, I'll shut them up."

That was our Janice. Jacki and I were stunned by the sudden change. Really? That was all it took? All Janice needed was to hear us say that we cared for and loved her? Wow!

Janice stayed at South Simcoe, excelled in grade eight and went on to high school. We made no threats or pleas, and we painted no glum pictures of a life ruined without an education. That wasn't what Janice needed. She simply needed to know that she was loved and valued, that she mattered. Who doesn't want that?

Once again, a student had taught the teachers. It wasn't enough for us to provide academic instruction; we also needed to provide mental and emotional support. Care and love do indeed provide a strong foundation for learning.

After the meeting with Janice, I began to apply the lesson over and over again. In fact, just a few days later, one of the teachers began describing her troubles with a particular student who just didn't seem to care about school, about life, about anything.

"He needs to know you care about him," I advised the teacher.

"But I do," she replied.

"Then tell him," I said. "He needs to hear it. Believe me, it works. Let your students know in some way every day that you care about them. If you're not comfortable about saying it to the entire class, then say it to one child a day. But say it."

It never failed to work at our school; our students craved the comfort of knowing that someone cared about them. They had to hear it spoken aloud. "We care about you and we love you." We all need to hear it in our lives; the children of South Simcoe simply needed to hear it more often.

Sometimes a student's anger and frustration would suddenly develop into a dangerous situation without warning. When this occurred, we had learned a number of strategies to diffuse the situation, along with good judgement and basic common sense.

Kim Kelly was a grade seven teacher, and nothing in her experience prepared her for the day when Carl, her student, exploded in anger, withdrew a rusty razor from his pocket, stared her in the eyes and said, "I have a razor...I'm going to get you."

Kim was having an end of the day chat with Carl about his behavior in class. Although the classroom door was open, she was alone with him; what was she to do? He was standing between her and the door so she couldn't run from the room, or reach the intercom to call for help. Instead, Kim had to think on her feet. She stood her ground while the boy waved the razor at her. She remained outwardly calm and said softly, "Please stop and think, Carl; we have talked about making good choices. Think about the choice that you are making right now. You can make a better choice. Yes, you did misbehave in class, and that's why we are here talking. That's a small problem, and we will deal with it—you know we always do. Let's keep the problem small;

put down the razor and let's work this out together. I'll help you."

Fortunately for Kim, the time that she had taken to build a good relationship with Carl (such an important and often overlooked strategy when dealing with behaviorally challenged children) had paid off. He was beginning to trust her and, as she kept talking quietly, her message began to sink in. Eventually, Carl put the razor away. Kim quickly alerted the office, and then she quietly resumed her chat while waiting for me to arrive. We did have to involve the police, and since Carl had serious mental health issues, he eventually had to be given specialized assistance in another facility.

When reviewing the situation and discussing alternate responses, Kim admitted that she thought that he was going to kill her. We invited the police to talk to us about effectively handling this type of occurrence in the future. The police were always so helpful in cases like these.

Years later, when we were reminiscing together about our time at South Simcoe, Kim said that she learned so much from this incident that no student could ever intimidate her again. She went on, "What I liked most about my years at South Simcoe, was being part of such a wonderful team, and how each one of us was a leader in our own individual way. We were all so dedicated to helping our students. We shared resources, we exchanged ideas, we laughed together, we cried together, we ate together—we ate together a lot; there was always food and celebration. We found the smallest things to celebrate, and that kept us going. I am so glad I had that experience, and I know we made a difference."

I was continuously being impressed by the teachers' creative yet practical solutions to problems. Sally Roberts, for example, was an enormously gifted and dedicated teacher, with a knack for encouraging her grade three students to face their fear and tackle difficulties. When Greg was afraid of putting anything down on paper (his hands would literally shake), Sally decided that a bit of fun might work, so she made a game out of the writing process.

They took turns speaking words out aloud, then seeing who could write them down first. Greg would start with a single word, perhaps "the," and they would write it down. Then Sally would say a second word, maybe "cat," and they would write it down. Next, it was his turn again, and so it went on until they had a complete sentence written down. They would continue to do this, and before he knew it, they had a complete paragraph. So simple, yet so effective.

Greg blossomed under Sally's warmth and guidance. By the end of the year, he was able to write a complete eight-paragraph essay on a tropical rain forest, a topic that had fascinated him during his social studies class. Individual attention, paired with Sally's determination to "find a way," along with her warmth and humor, all made such a difference.

Tom was a difficult student in Kim Kelly's grade seven class. Along with his disruptive behavior, he had difficulty reading; he said he couldn't. Were the two situations connected? I have no doubt they were. Tom's struggles to read at the same level as his classmates made him feel insecure and a failure, and soon he refused even to attempt reading. Nothing seemed to work until, one day, Kim overheard Tom speaking with great enthusiasm about fishing.

The next day, Kim arrived in class with some fishing magazines. She read an article to Tom, then had him read it with her and then stood back and watched him reading article after article. Tom was so interested in the fishing information that even though he couldn't read all the words, he forgot all his reluctance about reading. Kim had struck gold; she had discovered what motivated Tom.

To Tom, fishing was one of the greatest things he had ever experienced. Although he had only been fishing once in his short life, he had been successful. He had caught fish after fish, while many of the adults on the boat didn't catch any. He loved the feeling of success. Reading fishing magazines in class wasn't work; it was fun, and it reminded him of his success, so he made an extra effort to figure out unfamiliar words. He would ask Kim for help when he needed it, and he even used a dictionary.

Tom's initial fishing experience had given him a taste of success; he knew what it felt like to be a winner. Kim was able to use the fishing magazines to link him back to those great feelings, and use this as an entry point to help him to become a successful reader.

Jacki had a knack for winning students to her side. She would use pet names when addressing them—David would become "Davey," for example. It may seem like a small, silly thing among all the other teaching methods available, but the children appreciated her nicknames for what they were: terms of endearment, a kind of shorthand that said, "I like you. You matter to me. You are a good kid."

Few of us tire of being told we are loved, that we matter, that someone cares about us. To children who might rarely, if ever, receive those messages at home, Jacki's simple use of pet names was a tonic, and another reason to value and enjoy every hour spent at South Simcoe.

We had become more than a teaching staff. We had become a vibrant and highly functioning team, and the difference between the two is much more than just semantics. Not only were we personally and professionally committed to making a difference to the students at South Simcoe, we had grown to care about one another, personally and professionally.

"The South Simcoe Smile" was a manifestation of our caring. We had a smile for everyone, for each other, for parents and visitors, and most importantly, for our students. We vowed to keep on smiling in spite of whatever challenges we faced. Smiles are contagious, and soon we became known as "the school where everyone is always smiling," and the description included both the students and the staff members. Our smiles were never forced; we felt good about what we were doing, we knew that our efforts were paying off and we knew that our students and community were benefiting.

The family atmosphere at the school deepened with time. At the end of one school day, a student burst into my office to announce that the Prime Minister had arrived and was sitting in his limousine right outside the front door. The Prime Minister of Canada? Had our fame spread so far and so fast?

I followed the boy down the hall to the door and, sure enough, a white stretch limousine was parked at the curb, the motor idling and a uniformed driver behind the wheel. The children could barely contain their excitement, climbing on the hood and trunk, stroking and sniffing the finish—one child was even licking the car! They had never seen such an impressive vehicle. If the Prime Minister was not inside, it had to be some celebrity, maybe even an entire rock band—the car was that big!

I knocked on the window to see who was inside. When the window rolled down, I was surprised to see not the Prime Minister but Kim's boyfriend grinning at me from the back seat. He had a special surprise for her, and I had a good idea what it might be. When she finally emerged from the school and climbed into the limo, the children all cheered as they drove away to a special dinner, where her boyfriend proposed to her.

We all joined in the preparations for the marriage, planning teas and choosing gifts as though it were our own sister and not just a member of our staff who was being wed. Later, when Kim was hospitalized for over three months while pregnant with her first child, at least one staff member visited her or called once every week.

We took the same personal interest in other teachers as their own children were born—the children became "South Simcoe babies"—and we shared in the joy of their arrival.

Our family was growing.

As time passed, we realized more and more the impact we were having on our students—sometimes with touching results.

One day in the middle of an otherwise uneventful afternoon, Sally came into my office. Her face was white, her hands were trembling and she looked as though she were about to burst into tears. "Oh Sandra, I've done something terrible," she said. Sally was a wonderful, caring teacher, one of our strongest team members. I urged her to sit down, handed her some tissues and asked her to tell me what had happened.

"I told a student to shut up," she confessed. "I said, 'Please, shut up!' But still, it was 'shut up!' and I feel so badly about it. I can't believe I said it." Shut up had become the 's' words at South Simcoe, so telling anyone to shut up was a no-no. It was a violation of the basic principle of mutual respect, and a dishonoring of one of our respectful relationship agreements. Students had agreed not to say it to teachers, and teachers had agreed not to say it to students. Sally knew this, and nothing I said would make her feel any better—or any worse.

Once the words were out of her mouth, Sally realized that she had spoken before thinking. She took a deep breath and told the class she needed some time to calm down. She then left the room to regain her composure. I reminded Sally that she was a wonderful teacher; she had simply been frustrated and made a mistake. "We all make mistakes; you know that. Stay here until you feel ready, and then go back to your class and explain the situation to your students; tell them exactly what you told me. They are going to make mistakes too, and this will be an opportunity for you to model how to deal with a mistake."

And Sally did. She apologized to her class and explained that out of frustration, she had made a disrespectful comment and this was a mistake. She then asked the class to help her decide how to best make amends. When she finished speaking, Amy, a seven-year-old in her class, proved that our students were as understanding as their teachers. She said, "It's all right, Miss Roberts. You made a mistake and you have apologized. We will brainstorm with you, ways of better handling your frustration so it doesn't happen again.

Sally, as she explained to me later, didn't know whether to laugh or cry. When students begin to teach what they are learning, you know they understand.

Experiences such as Sally's confirmed that we were on the right path.

With the installation of large new windows, our rooms were now filled with sunlight. Plants and flowers added to the ambience. Motivated by our successes, we began to create team rituals and practices, which provided the psychological and emotional support we all needed to keep us focused on the positives. These later became known as "heart builders."

We created a "Bouquet Board," on which staff members wrote compliments, notes of congratulations and thank yous to one another, recognizing and celebrating achievements with students, events in their lives and little favors performed. Above the Bouquet Board, bejewelled "stars of success" highlighted the many successes we achieved as individuals and as a team within the school and the community.

We all loved coming into the staffroom to read the positive comments and share in the successes of our team. These demonstrations of caring energized us to continue our work, and made us a stronger team. They were the glue that held us together in the tough times.

Like all families, we encountered crises. And like all supportive and caring families, we helped one another through them.

When Michelle arrived at South Simcoe to teach, she was a great addition to our team. The students loved her bubbly and bright personality every bit as much as the rest of the staff.

Within a few months, however, Michelle began to have difficulties. First, she started forgetting things. Most of us would laugh off these incidents, saying we were all simply becoming too busy, or that it was due to stress and overload. But in discussions with Michelle, I found out her father had been diagnosed with Alzheimer's, and she spent many evenings and weekends caring for him. This certainly heightened her awareness and understanding of his condition, but caring for him as well as her preschooler, while looking after family obligations, placed intense pressure on her ability to handle the demands of everyday life.

Michelle's energy was drained, and this was having a negative effect on her ability to handle her teaching workload. Then, just when it seemed she couldn't possibly handle another source of stress, her marriage began to collapse. Her work was obviously affected; how could it not be? She felt she just couldn't cope anymore, and told me she felt her only solution was to quit teaching and get a job that was less emotionally draining.

I refused to accept that. I shook my head. "I can't let you quit," I said. "We are going to work through this together; remember what Sharon always says?"

She smiled and nodded. Sharon McLean often said, "We may crash from time to time, but we never burn."

"Michelle, you are going to get through this, and you can count on us; we are here to support you no matter what."

"Okay," she said, "I don't have the energy to fight. I'll stay if you'll help me." And, of course, we all did.

Michelle was a fighter, and she decided to take charge of the situation. With assistance from the Public Health Department, she began to access the help she needed. Caring for someone with Alzheimer's takes a toll on the caregiver, and can negatively affect their home and work life. Adults who are caregivers need support every bit as much as our students did.

We all gave Michelle our support. I would stop by her classroom twice each day to see how she was doing, what she needed and remind her how much she was valued and how many people cared about her. When passing her in the hall, I would give her a thumbs-up signal to lift her spirits. Every day, there was a compliment or two for Michelle on the Bouquet Board, treats would find their way into her mailbox and, to top it all off, she began receiving thank you notes regularly from her students.

Experiences like Michelle's strengthened our team and renewed our commitment to our students. "We can't give up on them," we would remind each other, " not even one."

Our refusal to give up on Michelle, had helped her to muster up the emotional strength to deal with her situation, and resulted in her becoming even more committed to helping her students succeed. "I'll never give up on these students. People didn't give up on me, and I made it, so they will too!" Michelle felt her experiences made her a better teacher and a better human being.

We proved it again: We needed as much support as our students did.

Another way of providing emotional support for staff was to begin our staff meetings by noting our successes and then ending on an uplifting note, by reading a passage from an inspirational book or a simple "thank you" note sent to the school. After an hour of discussion and solution finding, we were usually exhausted yet energized at the same time. It seemed appropriate to end these powerful sessions with a thought that recognized and reinforced the importance of "lighting the way" for the students entrusted to our care, and how spiritually uplifting this work was. This helped everyone to leave the session in a positive frame of mind.

Due to an overwhelmingly positive response to these readings and requests for more, we expanded this idea into what became known as our Wonderful Wednesday sessions. These were a great "heart builder."

These sessions were held at the lunch hour, for twenty minutes, when nothing else was planned. A group, whoever was available, would gather together in the staff room to chat, listen as someone read an inspirational passage or poem, or simply just reflect on how our work tested us on a personal as well as a professional level. We would explore strategies we could employ to keep us in a positive frame of mind as we pursued our dream of improving the lives of our students. We focused on topics such as dealing with personal stress and how it affected us as professionals, self-awareness, self-care and self-love, how to reframe negative comments from parents, how to deal with disrespectful parents and students who "pushed our buttons," and how to look after our health and well-being. Now and then, we invited people from outside the school who had expertise in these areas, to come and share their ideas and strategies with us.

We didn't stop there; we assembled a small library of books on personal development. We displayed affirmations in the staff room and around the school, which helped to keep us in a positive frame of mind and focused on the fact that indeed we were making a small difference in the lives of our students every day, and through our work we were making a contribution to society as a whole. Looking at the bigger picture strengthened us in ways that are difficult to explain.

Over the years, we created team rituals such as our end-of-the-term breakfast, held on the last day of every school term. We would arrive early, rain or shine, all decked out in our school colors, to eat breakfast together and celebrate our successes.

"The celebrations were inspirational, uplifting and unforgettable events; they had a huge impact on me. I remember standing proudly 'on the spot', sharing my successes and being applauded and congratulated by the entire staff. As a new teacher, this really encouraged me, and I felt such a deep sense of accomplishment and so supported. It made all the ups and downs worthwhile." said Mike Bowman to me, years later. Mike was a brand new teacher at the time and is now principal of his own school. We had a wonderful staff from different backgrounds and with many varied experiences. This was a great strength and gave us many differing points of view to consider when planning and making decisions. Let me tell you about my three very different experiences with Jacki, Randy and Frank.

Jacki Devolin was a classroom assistant, and she saw herself as a helper rather than a "real team member," so she was reluctant to voice her opinions or get involved in situations that she saw as "just for teachers," since she did not have a teacher's qualifications.

We all encouraged her, pointing out that every single person had a voice, was an important member of our team and had the right to make comments and give suggestions, as long as they were given in a respectful and caring manner. Easy for Jacki, she was the epitome of caring and respect.

It took time for Jacki to overcome her inhibitions, follow her heart and unleash her inner leader. Wow, the transformation was astonishing. Almost overnight, Jacki became everyone's big sister. We all, staff and students, felt comfortable confiding in her—including me, by the way—knowing she cared and would listen and offer her wise advice.

Jacki had a wonderful knack for organization, and no event at South Simcoe was launched without Jacki's meticulous approach to planning and scheduling. What a woman, what a leader!

In sharp contrast to Jacki, Randy Weekes needed a mere invitation to come to meetings and share his thoughts and opinions. Randy was the chief custodian at South Simcoe and quickly warmed to the idea of attending staff meetings, enthusiastically adding his ideas and suggestions. He and Gail, of course, had been the original inspiration behind our much coveted Golden Dustpan Award.

A dedicated environmentalist, Randy began doing small projects with the students to teach them about respect and responsibility for the environment. He would work with them to build birdhouses and bat houses, using recycled wood, and he created a small area in the garden with plants specially chosen to attract butterflies. Eventually, he formed an Environmental Club with students, teaching them about environmental issues and setting up a program for them to recycle paper, plastic, glass and other items (this was long before the idea became mainstream).

Randy made an impact across the city. When he saw the positive results of our gardening efforts at South Simcoe, he contacted all the other school custodians along Simcoe Street and suggested they plant gardens in front of their schools, using flowers in their school colors. A few years later, Mayor Nancy Diamond reminded me that, thanks to the leadership of our school custodian, "the entire city of Oshawa had grown more beautiful."

Jacki had been a classroom assistant, afraid at first to "act like a teacher." Randy was a custodian who could hardly wait to add his contribution to the students' education.

And then there was Frank. From the first time he heard me talk about turning the school around, Frank made no effort to hide his skepticism. "It can't be done," he would say, reminding me of the extra years of experience he had, as well as his deeper understanding of the community. "You just don't understand these people, not like I do. You have to be firm with these students; you need to get them to toe the line, suspend more of them and forget all this mutual respect stuff. Remember, I've been here for years, and I know things about this neighborhood that you can't even begin to know."

I suppose I realized from the start that Frank and I would not see things eye to eye. I was unable to hide my disappointment, and Frank could not conceal his animosity. The result was that neither of us handled the dispute as well as we might have, and Frank chose to transfer to another school at the end of that first year.

He wasn't the only one to leave in disagreement with me. Three other teachers chose to leave at the end of my first year, so I spent a good deal of time interviewing and hiring teachers to replace them.

I looked for compassionate and caring people whose enthusiasm and energy would inspire our students to do their best. I wanted people who felt as passionately about our students and their welfare as Sharon McLean did, those who would help to create a stronger and better functioning team, not just within the school but also with parents and members of the community. We finally selected three new teachers, and I am proud to say that they all made significant contributions to our work at South Simcoe.

Others would leave over the years, and the losses hurt me. Colleagues and friends had warned that this would happen; you cannot, after all, expect everyone to embrace major change with equal levels of enthusiasm. And I make no apologies for having high expectations for our students and being determined to do everything I could to help them to succeed in school.

Still, I regret losing the valuable experience that Frank and others might have contributed to our journey, and I wished I had the skills to inspire them and encourage them to embrace a new way of teaching and learning. Over the years as I developed more experience as a leader, I would reflect on this and say, "I would like to think that if only I knew then what I know now, I would have been able to redirect their efforts towards a different outcome.

How do you encourage, empower and champion others to develop their leadership?
To learn more about the power of the collective, sharing leadership go to my website: APublicSchoolMiracle.com.

Chapter 5

Extending the Teaching and Learning Team

With the school building spruced up and looking more attractive and welcoming, entry/dismissal and other necessary routines in place and working well, and more students showing up regularly and on time for school, we were all encouraged. These early successes were motivating and spurred us on to take the next steps.

I turned my attention to our parents. Their co-operation was essential. I knew from all the research I had read, as well as from my teaching experience, that when parents are engaged in the education of their children, and have high expectations for them, their children are more likely to succeed in school. I wanted for South Simcoe what I had experienced at Glen Dhu and other schools: parents who supported their children's learning at home, who encouraged their children's hopes and dreams, and parents who worked with the school to help us to better understand their children.

Once again, as principal, I received a harsh lesson in reality. Thus far at South Simcoe, parental attendance at school meetings was poor. Even the meetings that were more social in nature were not well attended. When we tried to make personal invitations over the phone, a technique that worked well for me in the past, many parents simply refused to answer telephone calls from the school. This seemed strange. I discovered that call display was carefully scrutinized before answering, and calls from the school were largely ignored. My immediate reaction, of course, was irritation—why would parents not answer a call from the school; what if it were an emergency? This had to change.

Eventually, I learned why. Many of the parents who would not answer the telephone were single mothers, and they used call display to avoid speaking to threatening or abusive former husbands or ex-boyfriends. Call display was a defense. In addition, if a child was exhibiting behavioral problems, some mothers didn't want to be asked to come to the school to retrieve their child. They had enough of their own problems to deal with and preferred that the school deal with problems created at the school.

When a mother saw that South Simcoe Public School was calling, she simply assumed it was bad news about her child, which she could do without. Even parents who chose to answer calls from the school, failed to respond in the manner I had come to expect. During our telephone conversation, some became non-communicative, reluctant to discuss any aspect of their child's schooling. Others were defensive and even abusive, actually shouting and cursing at me before hanging up.

I refused to be discouraged. I had seen how intelligent and promising many of our students were, and how quickly they were making improvements. I knew that with more involvement from their parents, they would make even greater improvements. I was determined not to give up.

We implemented a strategy I had introduced at other schools, making "Sunshine Calls" to parents. A Sunshine Call conveyed good news about the progress of their children, and every teacher was encouraged to make them. Remembering my mother's lecture about the unexpected Christmas doll, we all focused on finding something good to say about each child.

"It needn't be restricted to learning progress," I advised. Students could be praised for asking great questions in class, for demonstrating kindness and compassion to other students or simply for always making a good effort. This good news would serve as a conversation opener, leading to other discussions and thus building a relationship with parents.

The first few Sunshine Calls incurred suspicion, and even disbelief that teachers would phone parents to share good news about the results of a test or the completion of a reading assignment. Eventually, the calls became welcomed, especially when parents heard teachers say, "I just want you to know that I'm delighted to be teaching your child this year," or a similar statement.

As I suspected, word of our Sunshine Calls spread among

parents in the neighborhood. One parent would tell another that their child's teacher had called home, not to complain about Sammy or Emma, but to say how much they enjoyed teaching him or her. "How about that?" they might comment. "Isn't that different?" Even some parents with call display began to risk answering a telephone call from South Simcoe to learn that, yes, their child was doing well.

When contact between parents and school was no longer seen as a method of conveying bad news, conversations between teachers and parent became more pleasant, almost social in nature. Sunshine Calls proved to be an important strategy for building home and school relationships. The strength of this relationship over the years still astounded researchers, and frankly, continued to surprise me a little as well.

The foundational strength that this activity built, was due to the fact that in spite of all the challenges teachers were facing, they took the time to contact the parents of every child in their class by the end of the first month of school. This extended their work hours well into the evenings and weekends. Many of them made their Sunshine Calls from their own homes during the evening, when I'm sure they would have preferred to spend the time with their spouse and family, reading a book or just relaxing. But because they knew it would make such a difference to the students, they did it. I admire the commitment and dedication this required. Their attitude was the key to many of our South Simcoe successes, and to this day, I remain very proud of being a part of this team.

Now, I wanted deeper involvement from our parents. I wanted feedback and discussion on the changes we were making—I really wanted them to become engaged with their children's schooling.

I sent every South Simcoe student home with an invitation for their parents to gather at the school for a "coffee, cookies and conversation" meeting in a few days' time. I anticipated a turnout of perhaps twenty parents, which would make a good-sized group for discussion. On the day of the meeting, I arrived early to make pots of coffee and set out our snacks. At my previous schools, these sessions were always well attended, with some parents inviting friends along as company.

The time for our get-together came...and passed. No one arrived. They may just be late, I thought, and I stood at the window looking this way and that, up and down the street—but not a parent appeared.

I asked Joan if she had any messages for me from parents. Didn't anyone at least call and send their regrets?

Not one.

I sat and drank three cups of coffee alone. What had gone wrong? Were the parents so unconcerned about their children that they couldn't be bothered to attend a meeting? Later, I discovered that parents in our neighborhood looked upon "being invited to the principal's office" as a sign of "being in trouble." So it's no wonder they chose not to respond. Who wants to spend time in a school being scolded by a principal or hearing bad news about their children?

I decided to persevere; it was too important an issue to let it go. One morning, I went out into the schoolyard and spoke to parents as they were dropping off their children. I wanted to explain to as many as I could, that coming to meet me and chat with me did not mean they or their children were in trouble. I approached one mother and invited her in, and she agreed. I was encouraged. So this was all it took, I thought, a personal face-to-face invitation. I went up to another, and her response was frankly rude.

"Why should I talk to you?" she said. "I've got better things to do."

The next woman was just as brusque. "Leave me alone," she said. "I don't want to see you. I'm not in trouble."

Another woman told me that she didn't want to talk to me because she didn't have a problem. "But when I do," she warned, "you'll be hearing from me!"

Some parents, thank goodness, heard me out, and out of perhaps two dozen that I approached, three agreed to come inside for coffee and a chat. But even they were suspicious of my motives. "Why are we really here?" one parent asked.

I began by asking them to get more involved with the school, reminding them of our motto, "Together We Light the Way." I explained that we had put a great deal of effort into sprucing up the school so that it would be a warm and welcoming place to learn. I spoke about improving teamwork and leadership skills, and why we needed to increase academic achievement, as well as overall success in school.

Seeing the interest on their faces, I kept going, explaining that in terms of behavior, we didn't want fighting or any other form of aggression; we wanted a school where students felt safe and learned how to develop respectful relationships and to work as one large team.

I stopped to catch my breath and asked, "How do you feel about all this? Do you have any suggestions for us, any ideas about how to better help your children? You are their parents, and you know them best."

There was a long silence before one woman said, in genuine surprise, "You mean you want our opinion?"

I told her I certainly did.

She began with a list of all the things she did not like. She did not like the way students were free to walk around the room, and she did not like the idea of students working in groups instead of sitting in rows and concentrating on their work, which was the way she had been taught.

I patiently explained that students learned in different ways and that we taught them using a variety of models, strategies and techniques. When they were moving, they were not wandering about their classroom willy-nilly; they were learning co-operatively.

Working in groups allowed the students to learn and practice academic as well as social skills. They learned how to work together as a team, how to listen to and respect the ideas of others, how to see issues from different perspectives and how to put all their good ideas together to come up with the best solution.

I kept the explanations simple, and saw how keen the parents were to learn about all this. I was relieved; they were, after all, interested in what went on at the school. I proposed that we meet on a regular basis to continue this type of discussion.

"How often?" one parent asked.

I asked how often the group felt would be both necessary and convenient. We agreed on once a month for one hour. One parent suggested we might want a name for these meetings, and another said, "How about Parent Rap?" Parent Rap it was. We agreed that this gathering would be a forum for discussing and exchanging ideas about raising and educating children, an opportunity for everyone to become involved in decision-making and a chance to solve problems that affected the school as a whole.

It would not be a forum for discussing teachers and individual students. If someone wanted to talk about their own child, this would be handled by making an appointment with the teacher or with me.

An hour had passed and no one seemed in a hurry to leave, so I suggested they remain and discuss their children's education for as long as they liked. They stayed two hours, sipping coffee, discussing the challenges of raising and educating children, and gradually warming to the idea of becoming more involved in decision-making regarding the school's activities.

Although the group was small—I had recruited only three parents at this point—I was elated at the kind of discussion we began during that first session. I made Parent Rap meetings a top priority, missing only two due to ill health during all my years at the school.

At one session, a mother who was joining the group for the first time arrived, extremely upset with me, and when I asked why, she began explaining.

"I ordered my daughter to finish eating her food," she said, bristling. "When she didn't, I got angry with her and told her she damn well better effing finish it. And do you know what she said? She said I had no right to swear at her like that. She said I was being disrespectful to her and that SHE had the right to be respected. Can you imagine? My own child! I am her mother! When I asked her who the hell had given her that idea, she said it was you, Mrs. Dean!" Pointing her finger in my face, she continued, "She said that everyone has the right to be respected regardless of their age, and furthermore that no one has the right to yell, swear at children or be abusive in any way. I am her mother; I have the right to tell her what to do. Explain yourself lady!"

The mother narrowed her eyes. "Is that the kind of crap

you're teaching here, telling kids not to listen to their parents?" she demanded. I was taken aback at her anger, but I remained calm and said, "As a matter of fact, it is. Let me explain."

To my great relief and satisfaction, the other parents began speaking up, explaining how respect for everyone was the foundation for all we were trying to accomplish at the school. If you respect children, they will in turn respect you, they told her.

It felt good to hear them say those words. Their reaction was one more measure of the way we were starting to change the culture at South Simcoe.

Despite their comments, by the end of my first year at South Simcoe, I began wondering if Parent Rap was worth the effort we were putting into it. The monthly sessions, combined with Sunshine Calls, were helping to build relationships with parents, but they were not bringing large numbers of parents and caregivers into the school. I wanted to reach more people. I knew that I needed to generate a wider base of support.

"Do you really think we should continue with these meetings?" I asked at the last Parent Rap session in June. "I do a great deal of planning and preparation for them; this takes a great deal of my time, yet we still have only the three of you here for the sessions."

"Don't give up yet," one parent responded. "We love the time we spend here and the way we can talk so openly to you. We learn so much, and we have a better understanding of how the school works and how we can help our children to learn. And you have to admit, now that we speak our minds and help to make decisions, we also complain a lot less. Why don't we set a goal of doubling the attendance at Parent Rap by Christmas?" Now why did I not think of that? We agreed of course.

Parents demonstrated leadership by taking responsibility for spreading the word about Parent Rap sessions and recruiting people to attend. Parent Rap was fun, they told everyone. You get to enjoy coffee and snacks, and the principal is there to talk with you. You learn a lot about your child's education too. Wasn't that worth an hour a month?

By the end of the first term, we had exceeded our goal, and the group continued to grow steadily with every session. Discussions became open and lively, with a healthy airing of different opinions and different points of view. We confronted bothersome issues and dealt with them. This naturally led to a few tense moments in the early sessions. To keep the "feel free to speak your mind" atmosphere whilst still focusing on creating healthy and respectful relationships, and avoiding negative and disrespectful speech and behavior, we developed a series of relationship agreements (ground rules) for respectful and successful interaction.

Encouraged, I began collecting "thank you for coming gifts," small trinkets like pens, notebooks, small perfumes, aromatic soaps and coffee mugs. Participants loved receiving these. I also invited speakers from a number of organizations to discuss issues such as handling medical emergencies in the home, dealing with daily stress, bedtime routines, back talking and other topics. We always tried to respond to parents' needs. When they asked for help street-proofing their children, we invited a police officer to help us with strategies; when they said that report cards were difficult to understand, we changed the way we worded them, making them simple and easy to understand.

A range of speakers arrived at Parent Rap, and their topics would have done Oprah proud. The mother of one of our teachers, Tamara, was a retired bank manager. She arrived to explain how to prepare and manage a home budget. The Oshawa Health Department sent a nutritionist, who taught everyone how to shop for, plan and prepare healthy, low-cost family meals. She also explained the connection between good nutrition and brain alertness. Other speakers demonstrated how to read food labelling and how to get the most value for money spent at the grocery store.

Pamela Anderson, a banker from RBC, The Royal Bank of Canada, spoke to parents about getting off welfare and getting a job, the importance of understanding new job technology requirements and seeking a brighter future for themselves. When she invited parents to visit her in her gleaming downtown Toronto bank tower, to see firsthand what she was talking about, many accepted her invitation with enthusiasm.

We didn't always go outside the group for speakers. Some of the Parent Rap members had skills and knowledge of their own to share, and they did, with enthusiasm and an energy born from the knowledge that others wanted to hear what they had to say. When the government slashed social assistance payments later that year, it was the members of Parent Rap, along with our school social worker, who prepared a community directory of social services in Oshawa, places they could turn to for assistance. This directory was later adopted for use in the entire district—a great tribute to their talents.

We made it as easy and convenient as possible for parents to attend. Some parents, for example, could not afford babysitting fees and, therefore, were not able to attend. Carl told us that the local St. John's Ambulance organization taught babysitting skills to teenagers. So we invited them in to teach our older students, who then provided babysitting free of charge during our sessions.

Parent Rap had become a powerful relationship builder between parents and the school. Over time, parents became so powerfully motivated by being a part of our team, that they began to accept greater responsibility for the welfare of their children—how well prepared for school they were, if they had eaten breakfast and were ready for their school day, if they were getting enough sleep, if they were getting their homework done—and we could not have asked for more.

Parent Rap eventually created its own momentum in the community. Many schools, both in the catholic and public school districts, asked us to show them how. They invited the South

Simcoe parents to talk to their parents, and then began their own "Parent Rap" sessions. Can you believe it?

The leadership of our parents and the growth of Parent Rap throughout the community, we were told by the Mayor, significantly improved the quality of life throughout the city.

Veronica Lacey, the director of the North York School District (a very large and thriving school district) invited Parent Rap organizers to speak to her principals at the district's annual principals' conference. Joan Green, Director of EQAO, the standardized testing unit of the Ontario Ministry of Education, invited them to advise her as to how to report the results of the tests in a way that all parents could easily understand them.

Louise Brown, the education reporter for the *Toronto Star*, a large Toronto newspaper, featured them in a front page story. To top it all off, Parent Rap participants became such strong advocates for their school and community, and had such an impact on so many other parent groups, that they were cited in the provincial report from the Royal Commission on Learning, as a "success story and model for others to follow." Wow! Our parents had broken through the social and educational barriers that many parents from low income neighborhoods face, and had become leaders amongst their peers. What a tribute to their talents!

I began to wonder who was learning more from this experience—us or the parents. In spite of my beliefs about equality, I had to admit I arrived at South Simcoe with some preconceived ideas about the parents of the students. Among them was the possibility that the parents weren't taking enough responsibility for their children, and placed too little value on education. The underlying message was: *Why can't they just improve their lives? Then they could help their own children?*

This attitude is not, I'm sorry to say, rare among middle-class people who have never found themselves in situations of economic stress, or who have never been deprived of emotional support. It is very common for them to look at people—for example, those in the South Simcoe neighborhood—and ask, "Why can't they pick themselves up by their bootstraps and change the way they are living?" or "How can they choose to live the way they do?"

I often felt the same way. Until I met people like Sylvia. Sylvia's son, Mark, a grade four student, suffered from severe learning problems; he also seemed to be experiencing childhood mental illness. Mark could neither read nor write; and what's more, he didn't seem to care. Both Mark's teacher and I proposed that Mark be assessed for placement in a special class where he could receive the special assistance he needed. Try as we might, Sylvia refused to permit it.

I persuaded Sylvia to visit me in my office, where I planned to carefully explain the opportunity for more personalized teaching for Mark, in a much smaller classroom. It was the best solution we could offer Mark. But no matter how carefully I detailed the benefits for Mark, I could not persuade Sylvia to see my point of view.

Sylvia grew more and more adamant about refusing to send Mark to a special class; and I must admit, I became more and more frustrated with her. I simply could not understand why she did not want her son to benefit from this assistance.

Finally, Sylvia opened up with a tragic story that explained her reluctance, and forced me to reassess my perception of her and other parents. Sylvia told me that her sister, while still a very young child, had been diagnosed as mentally handicapped. "She threw a lot of temper tantrums," Sylvia said, "and she was hard for my parents to control. So they locked her up in an institution. She was just a little child, and they took her away to a home with other people they thought were crazy too."

Recalling her sister's story after all these years was painful, but Sylvia kept going. "When she was an adult," Sylvia said, trying to maintain her composure, "after she had spent all her childhood years in this home for the mentally handicapped, some doctors took another look at her case." Tears began streaming down Sylvia's face. "And do you know what they found out? They found out that my sister had never been mentally handicapped; in fact, she had a normal level of intelligence. She just had some severe hearing problems. She never should have been put away like that. But by then, it was too late."

I listened to her tale with growing horror. As a result of all the years confined in the company of truly handicapped people,

Sylvia's sister had acquired strange mannerisms that made others uncomfortable in her presence. Her sister had not been mentally handicapped when admitted, and she was not mentally handicapped as an adult. But she appeared as though she were, and her appearance and mannerisms were so disturbing that she could not be considered a candidate for early release.

"First, it cost my sister her childhood," Sylvia said through her tears, "and then it cost her freedom. And why? Because somebody looked at her as a little child and decided she should be put away from other children. Now do you see why I don't want my son placed in a special class?"

Of course I did. I didn't agree with her decision, but I now understood her opposition to the idea. Sylvia wasn't refusing out of stubbornness or ignorance to agree to his transfer. She was doing it out of love. She wanted to protect her son from risking the same horrible treatment her sister had received, because she could no longer trust the system to do the correct thing.

Sylvia's story brought tears to my eyes, and we cried together there in my office, with no embarrassment. I placed my arm around her shoulders. "Do you know what I see here?" I said. "I see a mother who loves her child very much. I thought you didn't care about your son. I'm sorry I misjudged you."

My words generated some trust in her, because Sylvia agreed that she would grant consent for us to apply for special assistance for Mark. This was a workable compromise since it gave us permission to formally request additional support for him. Mark eventually began to receive the educational assistance he needed, and we were all happier.

I think of Mark and Sylvia whenever I hear people discuss the problems of those who are mentally ill, handicapped or disadvantaged in some way. Many times, people talk as if these people created their own problems, or think that their problems are being magnified. They propose solutions that don't make sense. The situation is so much more complex than they realize. These people need different kinds of support—emotional, educational, financial, even political—in order to reach their full potential.

More and more, I began to appreciate the complexity of the issues facing the South Simcoe families. As a society, we applaud alcoholics who seek support from AA, drug addicts who go to rehabilitation facilities, and smokers who seek support to break the nicotine habit. But when support for the mentally ill in schools, and in the community in general, is proposed, the requests seem to fall on deaf ears.

We could have done so much more if we had more support for people like Mark and Sylvia. This is very sad, don't you think?

How do you ensure that 'parenting voices' are an essential element of the educational process in all communities? To learn effective strategies to increase 'Parenting Voices,' please go to my website: APublicSchoolMiracle.com.

Chapter 6

Creating the Village

My childhood in Trinidad was influenced, in one way or another, by our extended family as well as by our community. The African proverb, "It takes a village to raise a child," has become something of a cliché, but like many clichés, there is truth to it. Life has become far too complex for any single group to care for, nurture and educate children, and address all their needs.

When I grew up in Trinidad, we could always count on our neighbors for support when we needed it, just as our neighbors knew they could count on us. It was wonderful to grow up in this type of environment. Wouldn't it be nice if children everywhere could grow up with this kind of support from their extended families and communities.

In the South Simcoe neighborhood, these support structures were simply not there, and there was a kind of reluctance to become really close to your neighbors. Some of this, of course, was due to the transient nature of the community. It takes time to build relationships (children seem to do it so quickly and naturally!), and some families simply didn't remain in one place long enough to get close to their neighbors, much less count on them.

Nevertheless, our students were dealing with some pretty complex situations, and it was very difficult for their parents alone to care for them and address all of their needs. I was determined to do something about this.

More and more, our school was becoming the center of the community, a place where everyone came together and worked together for the common goal of helping students to succeed—why not take this to the next level and reach out to create an extended family for these students? An incredible opportunity presented itself.

As you've read, we had the beginnings of a powerful school team, and in order to maintain and sustain our team, we needed to be able to gather as a whole group, to hold school assemblies, concerts, and celebrations. We had no place but our hallways to do this, and here we had to squeeze in and stand; it simply did not work.

Wendy had made arrangements in previous years to hold the annual graduation ceremony at the nearby Legion Hall—why not build on the relationship she had established and ask if we could use the hall on a regular basis? I wondered.

After all, I heard that years before, when South Simcoe School was in the midst of a thriving community, the Legion manager Doug Finney's own child had attended the school, and because of this, he had a special appreciation for our efforts to restore the school to its former glory as it were.

Doug agreed to let us use the hall, reserving the right to review the situation each month. He asked only that we leave the hall as clean as we found it. Of course, we would—and did.

Once we had a place where we could gather as a team, hold school assemblies and celebrations and generally feel united as a school, our school family grew even closer. Meanwhile, Doug began spreading news of the school's achievements among the Legion members. Over time, the Legion members began to see our students not as kids who might wreck their hall, but basically as decent children who simply needed support, care and attention.

Once that idea took hold, they began reaching out to us. What did we think of some war veterans visiting the school on Remembrance Day, to talk to our students and tell them personal stories of World War II, the Korean War and other conflicts?

Naturally, we thought it would be wonderful: What a great way for our older students to learn how to interact respectfully with seniors, and to develop an appreciation for the sacrifices these men and others of their generation had made for our country. It would certainly bring history alive.

Their visits were followed by other offers from the Legion members, who donated stacks of *National Geographic* magazines and supported a wide range of school events throughout the year.

The creation of our extended family had begun; we had simply reached out to our neighbors and asked them to work with us to help our students learn, grow and develop in a healthy, safe and caring learning community.

This was the foundation for the development of all our school community partnerships, which forged an amazing bond between the school and the surrounding community, and led to us winning the National Partnership Award from the Conference Board of Canada.

We learned that four Kiwanis Club members had formed a band called "The Three Harmony Cats and a One Dog Drummer." We invited them in to play for our students, and pretty soon our kindergarten students began performing with them on their visits. The students sang along and accompanied the musicians with percussion instruments. The music from our intergenerational band may not have been concert-hall quality, unless you measure harmony and rhythm according to the level of joy it creates, but these performances were great fun for everyone involved, and the mutual joy created between people separated by several decades was something to behold

We began to receive many offers of assistance from the surrounding community, and we realized that in addition to background security checks, we needed to develop school and community partnership guidelines. We kept them simple; we wanted and needed community partners who understood our asset-based philosophy and our "extended family" concept of creating community partnerships. They had to agree to abide by our guiding principles. We knew that if we began our partnerships with the same mindset, we would be successful.

We wanted long-term partnerships; too many of our students had already suffered abandonment of one kind or another in their short lives, and we didn't want to impair their chances of success by adding to this risk factor of having new people move into their lives briefly before vanishing forever.

The Legion Hall was just to the north of the school. In the opposite direction, and directly across the street, sat a strip mall, and I remembered how my heart sank at the first sight of it. Malls represent tempting opportunities for students to get into difficulties, ranging from loitering to outright vandalism and theft. Even though we continued to make steady progress with improving our students' behavior, the mall presented as big a problem to us as many of our students did to the merchants.

Shoplifting by South Simcoe students and other youngsters in the community was a major headache for the store owners. Things grew complicated when the owners were both unable to contact the parents and reluctant to call the police. Invariably, they turned to us. Or more precisely, to me.

"You need to come and pick up your kid; we caught another one shoplifting over here," a store manager might say to me over the telephone. "It's about time that you put a stop to this."

The first few times I heard this, I took it personally and

became quite distressed, and perhaps felt a little guilty because I hadn't solved this problem. As time went on, I grew more and more frustrated, until one day when yet another merchant called to complain about "my kids." I slipped into my coat, marched across the street to the mall and entered his store. I try to control my temper at all times, but I must admit I was close to losing it on this occasion.

"Look," I said to the store manager, "I'm tired of being called to come and pick up *my kids*. They are not just *my* kids. They are *our kids*. They live in this community; their parents shop here, and they are every bit as much a part of this community as you are. So instead of expecting me to solve this problem on my own, why don't you help me?"

"OK," the manager said calmly. "What do you want me to do?"

His cool and helpful response was unexpected, and I was taken aback for a moment. The man was offering to help me solve a major problem.

"Well...I'm not quite sure; let me think about it and I'll get back to you."

Returning to my office, I gave the idea some thought. If we could partner with the Legion to solve the problem of space, why couldn't we partner with the mall merchants to solve the shoplifting problem?

We could and we did.

At first, we wanted to take the students over to the mall, but then we realized this was hardly necessary, after all—so instead, we invited the merchants into the school to plan how we could work together.

I approached the manager of the Swiss Chalet restaurant in the mall, a man named Phil Lawson. He would be, I feared, a hard sell. The students often amused themselves by loosening lids on his salt and pepper shakers, which caused many customers to return their meals. This and similar stunts created many headaches for him and his staff. But Phil surprised me by quickly agreeing to be involved. He said that we needed to put our heads together and come up with a plan to solve our problem.

At our first meeting, Phil suggested that he and the other mall merchants take turns coming to the school and talking to our students. He said that the mere act of crossing the street to meet the students in their own environment would make them feel important. This would be a good first move. He further added that when adults build good relationships with children, they usually treat them with greater respect. We all agreed that if the merchants were seen as friends, as neighbors, as people who cared about the students, they would interact with them in a more positive manner. The biggest concern they had was that the students might ask them some difficult questions; it was a school after all.

"If they do," I assured him, "I'll be there to help you answer them, assuming they're not too difficult for me as well."

Phil came first, and he was a hit! During his talk to our grade eight students, Phil talked about his business, his employees, the necessity for teamwork and respectful interactions, both with staff and customers, and how his love for entrepreneurship had led him to purchasing his own restaurant. He even suggested some of the students might own or manage a restaurant like his one day. "And if you do," he said, "I know you'll want everyone to treat you with respect." When he finished, the students swamped him with all sorts of questions, some amusing, some provocative and some rather profound.

Phil treated them all seriously, listening carefully and answering in detail. When the presentation concluded and the students returned to their class, buzzing with excitement about all they had learned, I posed a question of my own. What would he think, I asked Phil, about pairs of grade eight students actually visiting behind the scenes at his restaurant for short periods of time, to observe the teamwork and respectful interactions he had just described?

"Why not?" he said. "We can at least try it."

This became much more than an experiment; it grew into one of the most rewarding initiatives we launched at South Simcoe School. The children realized that teamwork was not just an idea cooked up by teachers to keep everyone organized and things running smoothly in the classroom. It was considered an important skill by society in general.

Teamwork applied even to something as simple as

assembling and serving a salad. It meant accepting responsibility for your task and trusting others to do theirs correctly, especially when the salad was to be served to several dozen people in 10 minutes' time.

They recognized that mutual respect was a most important value, and that respectful interactions were appreciated by all. They also began to gain an understanding of the intangible rewards meaningful work could bring. Might this help them to stay in school, join the work force and get out of the cycle of social assistance? Maybe...

I asked Samuel, one of the first students to visit the restaurant, what he enjoyed most. "It was fun, and it felt good; we made food and then watched people enjoy what we made. They ate it all, and they liked it," he said. "I wanted to go up and say, 'I'm glad you liked it...because I made it!'"

Before each visit to Phil's restaurant, the students were prepared by their teachers to observe how their school curriculum applied in the world of work. Phil took the time to explain how academic as well as social skills were important, and how everyone on the restaurant staff had to work together. To many students, it now made sense why we wanted them to learn math, language and so many other subjects, and why we wanted them to graduate with good marks. Schoolwork now became so much more interesting.

Very quickly, we saw positive changes take place on both sides of the fence. The small acts of mischief and vandalism at the restaurant virtually disappeared, because the manager and staff were now seen by the students as friends. Phil developed a special kinship with the students. It was no longer *your* kids, but *our kids*. "How are our kids doing?" he might say when we met. He also saw them as individuals, with special personalities and skills. "How's that little Sammy doing?" he would ask. "Boy, he asks a lot of questions! And how about Charmaine? She says she wants to be a waitress, but I told her she's bright enough to run this place."

Whenever Phil entered the school, students ran up to shake his hand and say, "Hi, Mr. Lawson! How's business?" Later, Phil arranged for the Swiss Chalet chicken mascot to participate in several events at the school. Whether it was the unusual sight of an adult-sized costumed chicken or the goodwill generated from Phil's support for the school, the Swiss Chalet chicken brought more than excitement and popularity with him. Whenever the chicken planted a flower in our garden, for instance, it was remembered by the students as "one of the Chicken's flowers," and received extra care and attention.

From this rather uncertain beginning, grew our program, "Connections: Classroom and Community," later used by many other schools as a way of students linking with their communities. As more businesses got involved, we maintained our focus on "creating the village," and developed relationships with individuals in the organization, rather than have a formal written partnership agreement with the corporation.

Partnerships with concerned and caring individuals varied widely, according to their situations. Some visited the school, working with our students, on a regular weekly basis. Others arrived less frequently, every few months perhaps, while many chose to work with us in a continuous advisory capacity, helping us with strategic planning and program implementation.

Our partners appreciated that instead of imposing our view on how they should be involved; we always began by discussing the larger goals of the school and asking how they would like to be involved in helping us to achieve them. The result was an amazing collection of skills, each adding its own unique dimension to our school.

Rob Pitfield, for example, an executive vice-president with Scotiabank, arrived to read stories to our younger students. Soon, his visits included relating tales of his successes and achievements, to grade seven students. The bonding between Rob and both groups of students was remarkable.

When Rob invited our grade one students to visit him at his office in downtown Toronto, they enthusiastically agreed and, on the scheduled day, were so excited that they couldn't wait, and they burst in on an important meeting he was chairing, with shouts of "Hi Rob!" They began telling the startled onlookers, "This is our Rob. He's our Rob; we love him. We brought a book for you to read to us Rob!" Rob, to his credit, accepted the interruption with his usual good grace and humor.

Another bank executive, Linda Sinclair, grew so impressed

with our programs that she also invited students to visit her in her Royal Bank of Canada office. Later, I was invited to speak to a group of Royal Bank's Ontario managers about our school's goal achievement process.

Terry Morgan, manager at the nearby T.D. Bank, helped our senior classes learn how to open a bank account, write cheques, balance a checkbook and establish and maintain a budget. Through their Friends of the Environment program, they assisted the school in planting and maintaining the lovely flower gardens that gave so many people so much pleasure.

Tom McNown, from the marketing division of General Motors of Canada, invited our grade eight class to GM's headquarters, where he showed them how the same mathematical skills they were learning in class were being applied every day by GM employees. And when one of the science classes at our school was having difficulty grasping the concept of fuel, propulsion and energy, Tom arrived in person to explain. I'm told that the students talked about his lesson for weeks afterward and, I suspect, will never forget it.

Barry Kuntz, with General Motors, arranged for his staff to provide a large tent at the school during our Community Celebration Day, where members of GM's Ontario zone arrived to read stories aloud to large groups of children who, of course, enjoyed this immensely.

Still with GM, Ann Nurse, owner of a local auto dealership, volunteered to speak to our students about the importance of teamwork and the role it played in helping her dealership provide satisfactory customer service. Ann also became a regular guest at our Circles of Love: Reading Together events.

It's difficult to exaggerate the value of these partnerships to our students. Many of our partners were busy senior executives, often with roots far beyond the South Simcoe community. They got involved because they believed it was important to contribute their time to those who needed it. Logic told the students that if these people felt it was important to spend time with them, then they must be important. The boost it provided to their sense of self-worth was immeasurable.

On a more practical note, our students who had never before been exposed to these situations, began to envision themselves finishing school and being in a variety of career situations. They now saw what they were learning in school as skills that were prized in the workplace and in society generally. The employees at GM, and in the banks, were making and analyzing graphs each day, just as they did.

They knew how to make decisions, relate to the needs of others, build and maintain relationships, and appreciate and accept differences between individuals. They could do these jobs too.

I'm the first to admit that this program did not spring fully conceived from my mind. As I explained, it grew out of a practical need to reach beyond the school itself, in search of assistance in helping our students to learn. No one, including me, could have foreseen the degree of its success. It generated such rich rewards for everyone concerned, and demonstrated the benefits to be gained when schools, businesses and communities work together to help children learn.

I wish I could say that after all these partnerships were formed, and the school and community were working so closely together, all our problems were eliminated, but things are rarely that simple.

On both sides, there was a growing understanding and co-operation. Our students were becoming more civic minded, and the mall merchants no longer treated them with suspicion and near outright hostility. But problems lingered.

One Monday morning, I arrived at school to discover that two grade eight boys had been caught shoplifting at one of the mall stores on the weekend. I called one of them—a cocky but, darn it, likeable boy named Jacques—into my office.

"Jacques," I said with great disappointment, "how could you do such a thing? You know these people now. They are our friends, our neighbors. They have come into the school and talked to us; they work with us and help us—how could you shoplift from them?"

Jacques looked bewildered. "Why are you so upset, Mrs. Dean?" he said. "Heck, it happened on a Saturday. School was closed."

I couldn't help myself. I burst out laughing, even as part of me wanted to cry. After all we had done, after all the progress we had made, Jacques and his friends still thought it was all right to shoplift as long as the school was closed for the weekend. We had a longer journey ahead than we first anticipated.

When we dealt with one problem, another seemed to pop up to replace it. In spite of Jacques's transgression, shoplifting involving our students had been non-existent for a few years.

Then there was more... We received a report of unacceptable behavior from the weight-loss clinic in the mall. The clinic's patrons, who were already self-conscious about their weight and appearance, began complaining to the owner of the clinic. They reported that some students were making rude remarks to them, standing at the clinic door—they would hurl insults at them: "Pig!" and "Fat cow!" were just two of the comments made by the students.

This was so upsetting to the patrons, and so damaging to the clinic that the clinic operator began circulating a petition to have all South Simcoe students banned from the mall. To add fuel to the fire, we learned that the same students were causing problems at the blood donor clinic in the mall. I was horrified, after all our work!

We had to act quickly. So, once again, I turned to Phil Lawson, the manager of Swiss Chalet, and Peter Jefferson, the Kmart manager, for assistance. They quickly organized an evening meeting, inviting the mall merchants, our staff, parents and community members.

Phil had a natural diplomacy and was always able to see both sides of any issue. Many of the merchants arrived visibly angry.

"Something has to be done about those kids," the manager of the weight-loss clinic shouted, thumping her fist on the table, "something drastic. We cannot have them coming over here when they feel like it, abusing our customers and scaring them away; this is bad for business. I hear from others that they're stealing merchandise when our backs are turned, and generally acting as though they own the mall. "

Now, clearly, this was an overreaction, because we had by now discovered that it was a group of six boys who were causing all the problems.

Phil explained how his involvement with the school had solved all the problems he had with the students. "Since I started working with the kids, I don't have problems anymore," he said. Then his voice softened, and he added, "They're just kids. They belong to this community; they are the children of our customers. We can't condemn them; we have to get together and help them."

Phil's words were spoken with such deep sincerity, and as he began to relate examples of the positive results he had achieved, he began to win others over to his side.

"Maybe we can all find some way of working together. I mean the entire mall and the whole school, and do something for the kids," one of the merchants offered.

"If we can all pull together and work with the school, the kids will know we care about them, and maybe they'll be more respectful to us, like they are with Phil and Peter," another suggested.

"How about the Santa Claus parade?" It was the owner of the weight-loss clinic, the same woman who had earlier been so demanding of tougher discipline. The City of Oshawa sponsored an annual Santa Claus parade to officially launch the holiday season.

"Maybe we can enter a float in the parade, representing both the school and the mall," they suggested.

Almost everyone began nodding their heads at the idea. Everyone, that is, except me. I loved the enthusiasm being generated; and the fact that they wanted to do so much for the students thrilled me. But I had always emphasized the concept of work life harmony to my staff. Christmas, I knew, was a stressful time; there were so many demands on everyone's personal as well as professional time. At school, we had report cards, interviews, concerts and staff gatherings. At home, there was always so much to do at that time of the year. I was afraid they were putting too much on their plates—the parade was less than three weeks away, and there would be so much work to do.

Before I could voice my concerns, the proposal took on a life of its own. With everyone contributing ideas, it was agreed that the South Simcoe float in the city's Santa Claus Parade would be a joint production by the school and the mall. Everyone seemed enthusiastic and confident. "We can handle the workload," Kim and Tamara assured me when the meeting ended. "We really want to do this!"

I was always saying to staff and students alike that they should dream big and focus on making their dreams come true. Everyone else saw this parade as a dream to bring into reality: the school and the entire mall working together. I still had serious reservations about time and extra work. My reservations were dispelled, when Rob, Kim's husband, an enthusiastic amateur pilot, took a leading role and managed to obtain some hangar space at the local airport, where the float could be constructed.

Every evening for two weeks, the staff, students, mall merchants and members of the local Kiwanis Club pitched in to design and build the float, working in the unheated airplane hangar. That year, the Oshawa Santa Claus parade featured a joint presentation from the mall and the school, with students waving and cheering from the back of a large flatbed truck—decorated with a giant banner: "School and Community Partnerships."

The meeting, which had been called to find ways of splitting the mall and school apart, actually produced a method of bringing them closer together than ever before, working in partnership for the education and well-being of the students.

As the number of our community partners grew, we were careful to involve people who saw helping to educate children as their social responsibility. This was the type of role modelling our students needed. Whenever we discussed working with a potential community partner, our first question was, "What's in it for our students; how will they benefit from this partnership?"

From a partner's perspective, their contributions produced wonderful, often unexpected rewards. The students at South Simcoe were not too "cool" to hide their appreciation, and their openly expressed joy made partners feel needed and important, which in turn encouraged them to spend more time with the students and explore more ways of lending assistance. "The smiles on the faces of those kids when they see me," one man told me, "is something I have never experienced anywhere else. It keeps bringing me back."

Our remarkable success with inspiring our students to do better academically, and engaging them in all aspects of school life by reaching out beyond the school walls, encouraged us to explore new ways of helping them to be even more successful. Many of them felt they would never make it in life because of their family background and circumstances, so we decided to show them that making wise and responsible choices could alter the course of their lives. We developed "The Choice Is Yours" program.

We sought out successful people who, even though they had grown up in situations very similar to those faced by many South Simcoe students, had triumphed over their difficult circumstances and become success stories. We invited these individuals to the school to share their personal stories with our students.

"Don't exaggerate, and don't try to whitewash the things you went through," we advised the speakers. We explained that our students were streetwise with realistic views of the world. "They don't need horror stories; talk to them about the challenges you faced, good and bad, the choices you made, good and bad, and how you learned from your mistakes and got to where you are today. Just be totally honest and upfront."

One of the most popular speakers was Zanana Akande, minister of social services with the Ontario provincial government at the time. While the students may not have fully realized all of Zanana's responsibilities, they recognized that she played a vital role in managing many important affairs, so they were taken aback when she asked, "How many of you have to study in the bathroom because there is no other private place to read or do your school work?"

Most students in the audience raised their hands. "Well, so did I," she said. "But I did not let it get me down or stand in my way, and you should not either. Always remember that the seeds of success are within you. I succeeded; you can too!"

They immediately warmed to Zanana, because she understood them. They began to pepper her with all sorts of questions, even asking her age. When she told them, they gasped. Of course, all children in their early teens assume that anyone over thirty is a dinosaur. In fact, the next question was, "What kind of cream do you use on your face to keep your skin looking so young?" This sent the province's minister of social services erupting into gales of laughter.

She was still chuckling when she bid me goodbye at the end of her visit. "Here I was, ready to answer all kinds of questions about my work and the government and such," she giggled, "and some kid wants to know what kind of face cream I use. It just made my day!" Zanana was so taken by the students, and they with her, that she invited them to visit her at her office in the provincial legislature a few weeks later.

Our students began to look forward to these sessions; they loved the casual and relaxed manner in which these very important people interacted with them.

Richard Irish, a business partner from Investors Group, made it possible for Robert Esmie, an Olympic gold medalist, to visit our school. He came bouncing down the hall as though strolling on the beach and, spotting me standing near a doorway, sashayed up, gave me his broadest grin and said, "How yuh doin? You smell sweet, girl."

"Thank you, and welcome to South Simcoe Public School," I replied. "You must be Robert Esmie. Allow me to introduce myself." In my mock-stern voice, I said, "I am the principal."

Robert quickly grew sober and apologetic, like one of our grade six boys who had been caught being naughty, until I convulsed in laughter.

His message to the students was similar to other speakers in the program. Flashing his gold medal, won at the 1996 Atlanta

147

Olympics, he told them that winning the medal was the fulfillment of a dream he had when he was their age, growing up in the rough Northern Ontario mining city of Sudbury. Robert and his friends all had dreams, and they shared them with one other. One boy wanted to become a doctor, another a teacher, and still another dreamed of becoming a karate master, opening his own school and maybe appearing in movies. Robert, of course, wanted to win a medal at the Olympics.

Here was the core of his story: *No one laughed at the others' dreams.* In fact, they all promised to help one another achieve their dreams as they grew older, and they actually did. Even when some moved far from the city, the boys kept in touch, reminding one another of their dreams and how important they were. "And you know what?" Robert said. "We all made our dreams come true. We all became who we wanted to be. We never gave up."

The children sat enthralled. Here was an honest-to-goodness hero, describing all the hardships he had suffered as a young child, first growing up in Jamaica, where he had to share a bed with his two brothers, and later training steadily for days on end, often alone and with no promise of success, just to make his dream come true.

"You can become anything you want to be," Robert said, "from a sports hero to an A-average student. The important thing is to have a dream, commit your heart and soul to it, treasure it and do the things that will help make it real someday.

People may scoff at your dream," he warned them, "but that doesn't matter. You have to keep believing in it, and believing in yourself and your own power. Your biggest supporter," he said, "has to be you."

From others, it might have sounded like just another pep talk, but Robert himself had put up with laughter from others about his dream. When he graduated from high school, Robert was a scrawny, 115-pound kid who slept with a relay baton in his hand every night so it would become as much a part of him as his own hand, and so he could fall asleep dreaming of running the perfect relay race. "I began working out to build my muscles," he told the students, "and kept finding ways to run faster. And here I am today."

Then he displayed the same baton his relay team had carried to win the Olympic gold medal. "And here is the baton I used." Nobody, of course, was laughing at Robert now. He didn't sugar-coat life for the students. He knew the kind of hurdles these students would face, because he had encountered some himself. They were bound to face temptations, like drugs, that could pull them away from their dreams. They had to recognize these temptations for what they were: barriers to making their dreams come true. They had to use all the problems they encountered, and overcame, to make themselves stronger. "Don't ever forget where you are coming from," he advised them, "and always know where you are going."

Later, he let every student hold his precious Olympic gold

medal. "Make a wish when you touch it," he suggested. I will never forget the expressions on their faces as they closed their eyes, made their wish and imagined their dreams coming true in the presence of a real-life hero.

Another speaker, Dr. Roland Hosein, was pleasantly surprised to learn how aware our students were of environmental issues and their responsibility for the environment. Dr. Hosein was the vice-president of environmental health and safety for General Electric Canada.

As soon as the students learned that he dealt with environmental issues, they began grilling him about his company's commitment to recycling materials and reducing pollution. Intrigued by technological advances in environmental matters, they surprised and impressed the GE executive with their awareness of issues and their leading-edge ideas, such as launching an inter-scholastic internet-based dialogue on environmental issues; and needless to say, GE became another long-term partner.

When the federal government of Canada later provided funding for our programs, to be implemented in schools across Canada, we also received, from the GE Fund, their largest philanthropic grant ever made to a school system.

Dan Carter, a local broadcaster and former actor on the popular Law and Order TV show, visited. He discussed his struggles with grief, drugs, alcoholism, abuse and dealing with undiagnosed dyslexia. He was honest and forthright about his mistakes and told the students how he worked every day to improve himself. They were amazed by his honesty. (Dan Carter went on to become the Mayor of the City of Oshawa.)

My friend, Lucy Greene, whose company had provided us with new furnishings when we so desperately needed them, also arrived as part of "The Choice Is Yours' program. Born into an immigrant Ukrainian family and now the mother of six children, Lucy had earned her MBA while in her mid-forties and had risen to a top executive position with Sun Life.

"And you know what?" she told the students. "I couldn't even speak English when I started school. Not a word!" Like many immigrant families, Lucy's had emphasized, over and over again, the importance of obtaining an education, and Lucy had taken it to heart.

"It's not just a matter of working to improve your math or your reading scores," Lucy advised them. "Focus on making the choice to get better and better, to keep growing and learning and improving. Never stop, and never give up. You can do it, but you have to make the choice to."

Some of the senior students were so taken by Lucy that they accepted her invitation to visit her at her office, high in a gleaming skyscraper in midtown Toronto. For many of them, this was their first visit to the big city, and they were suitably impressed with her beautiful office; I was too. They were amazed that this warm woman, who had achieved so much success in her career, knew not a word of English as a young schoolgirl and yet had been able to achieve so much.

Over the years, many others participated in the program. Some were not as colorful or mesmerizing as Lucy, Robert, Roland and Zanana, but each provided our students with a sense of the world beyond their neighborhood, and the realization that others had dealt effectively with moral and ethical dilemmas and had overcome hardships similar to those they endured, and that they could too.

The opportunity to meet all kinds of professionals from various fields helped our students to understand and see some of the possibilities of life after school. These personal stories, told by adults who had refused to let their life circumstances define their futures, inspired our students and helped them to understand that while adversity is not what anyone wishes for, often our greatest growth occurs as a result of our trials—a lesson I too was learning.

How do you engage and unite your entire
school community towards a common goal?
If you would like to learn more about the power of creating
a shared vision regardless of diversity, please go to my
website: APublicSchoolMiracle.com.

Chapter 7

The Limits of Love

Many of the people who were interested in the changes at South Simcoe, were focused on the behavioral challenges we faced. I must admit that this was a huge issue for us at the beginning, and naturally a primary responsibility for me as principal. Among the behaviors were fighting, bullying, aggression, vandalism, shoplifting and the accompanying classroom disturbances.

"But these are not the causes," I always said to my questioners. I have never believed in merely dealing with problems at the surface level. After the immediate and necessary intervention, I prefer to get to the root of the problem and take steps to prevent it from re-occurring. Yes, this approach takes a great deal more time, energy and patience, but treating only the symptoms of an issue, guarantees that the underlying problems will resurface in another form, at another time. There is no long-term change.

More to the point: The headaches caused by our many "problem students" were offset by their wonderful response to our efforts to meet their need for attention, affection, respect and, yes, love. Sometimes the reaction of our students set us off laughing in unbridled joy. And sometimes the tragedy of their lives sent us off into a dark corner to weep in despair.

Here are just a few of the many South Simcoe students who needed love and care—the ones that still flood our memory with joy, sadness, hope and, sometimes, a twinge of regret.

We all suffer setbacks, injustice and pain in our lives. As adults, we learn to accept and deal with it. But children are not equipped to handle unfairness without distress and severe emotional scarring, and no one was more injured in this way than Maria.

Maria had so many strikes against her that it seemed difficult, at first, to imagine that her life could become even more tragic. But it did.

Maria's life was a nightmare. Besides watching her family struggle with unemployment and poverty, Maria had to endure the dual challenge of dealing with both a learning problem and being hearing impaired. She had been given a hearing aid to wear, but it embarrassed her, and she often removed the device, trying to get through classes without fully understanding all that was being said to her. To compound things, she wore the aid to some classes and not to others, so not all her teachers knew of her disability.

Maria had huge dark circles under her eyes and was always serious. On the rare occasions when she smiled, it was a bittersweet expression, like an attempt to conceal some hidden adversity. She also dressed in baggy clothes that enveloped her and added to the image of sadness.

There was more. Although she had advanced to grade nine, Maria's progress was so poor that, at her own request after consulting with a social worker and her high school principal, she was admitted to grade eight at our school. It made good sense, because Maria would receive the special attention she needed at our smaller school. But the blow to her already crippled self-esteem must have been devastating.

My first sight of Maria, looking so lost and forlorn, made me determined to help her succeed. We accommodated her hearing impairment in various ways, and assured her that we would do all we could to help her return to high school the following year. With luck and hard work, she would taste success after all, and we were pleased when she began to respond with better grades.

Then we discovered she was pregnant—as a result of a rape. Her attacker, Maria told us, had crept up behind her when she wasn't wearing her hearing aid. She did not hear him coming and, when it was over, she was too embarrassed to tell anyone about it. For months, she hid her condition; hence her baggy clothing, until it became too obvious.

I managed to avoid crying about Maria until I arrived home that evening, and then I let the floodgates open. Maria was barely into her teens, bedeviled by problems many adults would have difficulty coping with, and now this: a child having a baby.

What more could happen to her?

I discovered the answer a few days later.

One of Maria's friends, seeking to raise her spirits, loaned her a necklace to wear.

During the lunch hour, Maria was in the shopping mall, across the street from the school, when she encountered her friend's mother, a woman who knew of Maria's troubles and condition. Unfairly, the woman assumed that Maria had stolen the necklace from her daughter, and she attacked Maria, physically and verbally, in front of other students and several mall shoppers.

"You thieving little bitch!" she screamed, as Maria cowered against a wall. The mother demanded the necklace back, in spite of Maria's tearful explanation. "The only thing that's any good about you is what you have between your legs!" the mother shouted with unspeakable cruelty. "At least you can trade it for favors. Otherwise, there's nothing good about you, and there never will be, you little tramp!" Strangers stopped and stared, some with contempt, others with disapproval, all of it directed at Maria.

Maria returned to school in near hysteria, feeling more shame than anyone should be asked to bear. She poured her little heart out in my office between sobs. She had done nothing wrong. She was not a bad girl. Why, then, was all this happening to her?

I comforted her as much as I could, and then I called to invite the mother in for a chat and an explanation.

Even when the mother learned the truth, she refused to offer an apology. "She shouldn't have been wearing my daughter's necklace," was her best explanation. After she left, I sat wondering about a woman who would value a piece of cheap jewelry over the feelings of another human being. What kind of values was she teaching her own children? What kinds of scars would they bear through life as a result?

Maria had her child in May. The following month, she appeared back at the school, her month-old baby daughter in her arms, determined to write her final exams. Maria's mother, she informed us, was unable to babysit the child that day, and she knew that she could turn to us for help.

This posed a major dilemma for me. The presence of a month-old baby in the examination room was certain to be at least distracting to the other students. But I was impressed with Maria's resolve, and she obviously sensed my concern. "Don't worry," she assured me. "She's just been fed, so she'll be all right for an hour or so."

We could hardly refuse her. "I knew you all would find a way!" Maria grinned when we agreed to the idea. Kim watched over the little one while her mother wrote her grade eight final examination, and when some of the students finished their exams early, they volunteered to remain in the school, taking care of the baby in Kim's place. If I had any doubts about our success at creating a true family atmosphere at South Simcoe, they were surely dispelled.

As educators, we accepted that marriage breakdowns, economic disasters, parental addiction problems and a host of other risk factors seemed to counterbalance our efforts in the classroom. Even though these kinds of situations threatened to overwhelm everything we were trying to achieve with our students, we felt that we could continue to succeed, by helping our students to develop their sense of self-worth and inner strength, and thus become resilient. They would then be better prepared to face the various challenges of life. We had to help them deal with their crises and then use them as opportunities to learn new coping skills, practice new behaviors and then anchor or reinforce these new behaviors.

Leonard arrived at South Simcoe from Edmonton, enrolling in grade six during mid-term. An attractive, fair-haired boy with pleasant manners, Leonard seemed to fit in quickly. He made friends easily, and his school work was adequate if not spectacular.

Rather quickly, however, the staff and I noticed his strange, unpredictable behavior. "Sometimes when I'm talking to Leonard," his teacher told me, "he just isn't here. He's off somewhere, in a world of his own, and he doesn't hear a word I say."

I suggested to her that daydreaming was hardly unheard of among students of Leonard's age.

"This is more than daydreaming," she replied. "When I finally get his attention, sometimes he gets right to work, and other times he explodes in anger. He'll swear and shout, or throw a book across the room. He becomes very frightening, and then settles down almost as fast. It's as though he has two personalities, one sweet and the other scary."

It sounded as if Leonard was suffering from a serious psychological problem, so we made inquiries at his previous school in Edmonton. Had they any record of similar behavior during Leonard's years there? "No," the answer came back. He had been considered a pleasant, well-behaved youngster. I grew curious and concerned. Something had happened to change this boy's personality. Relocation is almost always difficult for an eleven-year-old, but Leonard's reaction seemed extreme.

I discovered that Leonard was living with his maternal grandparents in Oshawa, and I contacted them to chat about Leonard and his problem. Bit by bit, the causes of Leonard's behavior became clear.

Leonard had arrived at South Simcoe in a state of shock. Back in Edmonton, his mother, a single parent, had died suddenly. This was traumatic enough for any young boy, but the death had not been accidental. She had been murdered. As if that weren't enough, Leonard learned, through extensive media coverage of his mother's death, that she had been a prostitute, slain on the street where she worked. Leonard had loved his mother deeply and had no inkling that her evening "job" consisted of meeting strange men and letting them take her to hotel rooms for sex.

It wasn't just Leonard who discovered the truth about his mother, of course. His Edmonton schoolmates learned it as well and, as children will, began to tease him about it. When the pain became too much for Leonard to bear, a decision was made to send him east to live with his still-grieving grandparents. Leonard may have left the taunts of his school chums back in Edmonton, but he carried all his agony to South Simcoe with him. Knowing the cause of his suffering helped us to understand Leonard's extreme behavior. Nevertheless, there was worse to come.

One Monday morning, two boys about Leonard's age approached me in the hall. "Can we talk to you about Leonard?" they asked me. They appeared concerned, almost frightened.

Curious, I invited them into my office, where they stumbled over themselves to describe what had taken place over the weekend.

Leonard, it seemed, had invited the boys to his grandparents' house for a visit. "Do you want to meet my mom?" Leonard asked them at one point. Before they could reply, Leonard removed a ceramic urn from the shelf, carried it to them and lifted the lid. Inside were the ashes of Leonard's cremated mother. "Here," Leonard said handing one of the boys the urn. "That's my mother. Say hello to her."

When the boys pulled away in shock and horror, the urn almost slipped from Leonard's hands. But it was his friend's words that sent Leonard over the edge.

"Man, you're weird," the boy said. "You're totally nuts!

What's wrong with you anyway?"

"Are you going to hold her?" Leonard demanded. "Are you going to hold my mother or not?"

"No, I'm not!" the boy replied. He and Leonard's other friend looked disgusted.

Leonard set the urn aside, left the room and quickly returned carrying his grandfather's shotgun. "You hold the urn or you get out of my house," Leonard screamed, aiming the weapon at them. Naturally, they fled in terror.

"You have to do something about him," one of the boys said to me. "He's crazy!"

I was glad I had taken the time to discover something of Leonard's background. Leonard was not crazy. Hurt, confused, angry and feeling unloved perhaps, but not crazy. Of course, once the boys spread the story about Leonard's threat with the shotgun among other students, Leonard became more alone than ever.

Beyond providing as much understanding as we could, we knew we had to inform the police, as well as obtain more counselling for Leonard. The experience also provided us with a "teachable moment," an opportunity to help our students understand the pain other students were experiencing, and how empathy, compassion and love are needed at times like this.

Leonard became entangled in a custody battle and was returned to Edmonton shortly after the episode with the shotgun. We provided his new school with as much background information about Leonard as we could, and hoped he would receive the assistance he so desperately needed.

Leonard is out there somewhere, trying to deal with all his pain and anger. We just hope he is not dealing with it alone.

Cathy's case was similar to Leonard's in some ways. Cathy was the picture of innocence: large, bright blue eyes, silky shoulder-length hair and a mobile face that could change from deep, serious thought into a mischievous grin at the speed of light. I enjoyed speaking to her and seeing the glow of her smile appear, like rays of sunshine breaking through a cloudy sky. I loved hearing her read aloud in class, watching her beam with pride at her accomplishments, which were well above the level of most of her classmates.

One morning when Cathy failed to appear for her grade one class, we followed the normal procedures for our "Safe Arrival" system and called home to confirm her mother's knowledge of her absence. The woman's response sent waves of fear rolling through everyone. "What do you mean she's not at school?" she said, her voice already shaking. "I took her there myself this morning. I watched her walk into the schoolyard, and we waved goodbye to each other. *What do you mean she's not there now??!!*"

While waiting for Cathy's mother to arrive at the school, we asked other students in her class if they had seen Cathy arrive. One had, and her story was chilling. According to this little girl's account, Cathy had been in the playground before entering the school building, when a man appeared out of nowhere and carried her off. Fearing the worst, we began interviewing students in their classrooms, asking if anyone had witnessed Cathy's abduction. Two grade eight students had and, streetwise as they were, they provided a detailed description of the man.

"He was wearing a sleeveless black leather vest; he had tattoos on his arms and long black hair."

"He called her name, and she ran up to him and they hugged each other," the other student added. "Then he picked her up and carried her off. She wasn't kicking or screaming or anything."

"If she had," his friend said, "we would have said something or stopped him ourselves. We just thought he was her dad."

The teachers on yard supervision that morning had not noticed anything unusual. My fear, of course, was that the man may have taken time to learn Cathy's name and build her trust, so he could abduct her without causing a scene. I immediately called the police to report the incident, and was still talking to one of the officers when the woman we understood to be Cathy's mother arrived, near hysterics.

When she heard the students' description of the man seen with Cathy, and the police added that they had received reports of a suspicious man in the neighborhood, the mother held her head in her hands. "It's Phil," she said. "Oh my god, it must be Phil!"

The police asked who Phil was.

"Her father," she replied. "He must have gotten out of jail."

When I asked the woman who had custody and what rights she had regarding Cathy's care, she sobbed, "I don't have any rights."

Slowly, the full story emerged.

When Arlene, the woman who called herself Cathy's mother, first met Phil, he was caring for Cathy, who was just six months old at the time. Cathy's mother had been sent to prison on serious criminal charges, and Arlene and Phil soon began a common-law relationship. But Phil became involved in serious trouble with the law as well.

During one of his infrequent times out of jail, Phil assaulted Arlene, frightening her so much that she moved out of the home they had shared, taking Cathy with her. She had to; without Arlene, Cathy had nowhere else to go. Besides, Cathy considered Arlene to be her actual mother, and Arlene loved Cathy as though the girl were her own flesh and blood. By all reports, Arlene was a caring mother, doing as well as she could under the circumstances.

Convicted of trafficking in cocaine, Phil had spent much of the past four years in prison. Now it appeared he had reclaimed his daughter and carried her away, for reasons we did not understand, to a place we did not know.

"Would he hurt the child?" a police officer asked Arlene.

She shook her head. She didn't think so. In fact, she suggested, Phil had probably taken Cathy because, as her parent, he thought that he would qualify to receive social assistance payments.

The police were naturally concerned, but they were a little confused as well. The father had not actually kidnapped the child; he had legal custody, after all. They were just about to leave the school, promising to look for Phil and Cathy, when my telephone rang. It was Phil. I waved the police back into my office while demanding to know if Phil still had Cathy with him. He assured me he did, and that she was fine.

I could barely restrain my anger. "You could have had the courtesy to come into the school and explain who you were and what you were doing," I told him. "The police are here. We have been looking for Cathy, assuming she had been kidnapped."

His lame explanation was that he doubted the school would have released Cathy into his care. In that respect, he may have been correct, of course.

I handed the telephone to the police, who took down all the details of Phil and Cathy's whereabouts, and his plans for her. Phil planned to return home to Toronto, taking Cathy with him. She would be out of the school, out of our lives and, tragically, out of the life of Arlene, who had unselfishly loved and cared for the little girl for much of her life.

It didn't end there.

Arlene remained in my office, where she spent much of the day grieving for Cathy, spinning us stories of Cathy as she grew into a trusting and loving child. I suggested Arlene might be able to obtain legal advice based on her role as Cathy's surrogate mother, and I asked her to stay in touch with the school and keep us informed. When I called Arlene a few days later, she told me in a still-tearful voice that a legal-aid lawyer thought she had only a slim chance of winning custody; and in any event, it would require a long and probably bitter court battle. I assured her that we there if she needed us.

Later, when I realized we had not heard from Arlene for some time, I phoned the number she had left with us. The woman who answered explained that Arlene had moved away. No, Arlene had left no forwarding address, and the woman had no idea where Arlene had gone. We never heard from Arlene again.

But we did hear from Cathy. One day, I received a telephone call from the principal of a public school in one of the Western provinces. Cathy, the principal said, was a difficult child. She refused to speak a word to anyone—not to other students, not to the teachers. She had become very withdrawn. It had taken quite a while to track us down, and the principal was looking for some guidance in helping her come out of her shell. Cathy's father, Phil, the principal informed me, was back in jail, and the little girl was in the care of a new girlfriend.

My heart almost shattered at the news. Was this really our bright, precocious Cathy, the little girl who giggled at funny stories during reading time and sometimes skipped hand in hand across the playground with her friends? I quickly outlined her situation to the principal, then suggested she hand the receiver to Cathy. Perhaps she would speak to me.

When I heard her small voice say hello, I answered, "Hi Cathy. This is Mrs. Dean from South Simcoe. Do you remember me?"

Indeed she did. "Mrs. Dean," she answered. "Will you come and get me please?" She began to cry.

My eyes filled with tears. Summoning all my training to keep my voice calm, I told Cathy that we all missed her and we wanted to know how she was doing. Through her tears, Cathy assured me she was doing fine.

I just spoke with your principal," I said. "She seems like a very nice lady, and she likes you very much. So will you show her your very best work? And will you read to her from your book, the way you used to read to me?

Across all the miles of telephone wires, I heard her small voice promise, "Yes."

"Your principal will let you call here if you need to talk to us," I said, and we talked for a little while longer before saying goodbye. Hanging up the phone, I sat for several minutes reflecting on all the trust that children place in adults, and consoling myself that Cathy was in the hands of a caring colleague.

Every teacher's experience is a microcosm of life. But events of joy and sadness, triumph and tragedy, victory and loss just seemed to be drawn with sharper edges—literally, in one terrifying case—at South Simcoe.

Where children such as Cathy could melt your heart with one unexpected smile, Tom could harden your resolve with a single angry glance. Tom, a grade eight student, practically snarled his way through every day at school, terrifying the students and insulting the teachers. The various strategies we tried were not very effective, and when he made a particularly vicious comment to his teacher, Anne, in class one day, she sent him to my office for a one-on-one session.

I began by talking to him about his behavior and letting him know that it was unacceptable. Tom claimed he had done nothing wrong.

"Let's be honest here," I said firmly. "Was that a respectful way to speak to your teacher?"

"Why should I be respectful to her? She hates me," he said.

"She does not hate you." This teacher was as dedicated to her students as anyone in the school. "She loves her class. She cares about all her students."

"Yeah?" Tom sneered. "Ask her; she hates me. That's why I bug the hell out of her."

I called Anne and asked her to join us. "Tom is convinced that you hate him," I told her, meeting her alone outside my office. "He says that's why he is so obnoxious in the classroom."

Anne sighed, and shook her head. "You know what, Sandra?" she said. "I hadn't thought about it before, but I really do dislike him. I'm trying not to, but his behavior drives me crazy."

Although Anne had tried to conceal her feelings towards

Tom, he was able to sense them. Perhaps, I suggested, we could put our heads together to find something about Tom that she could relate to, some aspect of his personality she could find interesting if not appealing. Then we could build on that. (I was, of course, harking back to my mother's lesson to me about the Christmas doll.) "Try complimenting Tom when he does even the slightest thing well. Maybe he'll change his attitude and be more co-operative."

Tom agreed to start fresh and try to work with his teacher. Anne focused on the few things Tom did well and began complimenting him on them. She would congratulate him on the way he began a project, even when he failed to complete it. When she brought treats for the class, she ensured that Tom received the first one, and whenever she spoke to Tom, she placed her hand on his shoulder as a gesture of affection. Although Tom's behavior improved, he was still not as co-operative as she expected.

"What if we invited Tom's mother to the school? All four of us could discuss the problem, and perhaps a solution would reveal itself."

Anne was skeptical, fearing that Tom would continue his rudeness, but I persuaded her to join us for a meeting in my office. Tom's mother arrived the following week. She was a pleasant woman but somewhat guarded at first. The most remarkable thing I noticed was the change that his mother's presence made in Tom's personality. The tyrant of South Simcoe

Public School had been transformed into a model student; he was sitting silently next to his mother, listening intently as she spoke, and beaming with joy whenever she turned and gave him a smile.

Anne and I were both amazed at this change. Anne revealed to Tom's mother all the ways in which she had tried to persuade Tom that she cared about him.

"I like Tom," Anne told the mother. "I honestly want him to do well. But he can be very frustrating. He simply does not respond as respectfully as he should."

"He gives everybody a hard time at first," Tom's mother said. "It's his way of testing you, to see if you really like him or not. The trouble is," she admitted, "he usually gives people such a hard time that he turns them off."

I was amazed that his mother would admit this so openly. To her credit, she promised to work with us to try to change Tom's belligerent attitude. I couldn't persuade her to join us at Parent Rap, where I felt we might make real progress, but both Anne and I noticed a change in Tom once his mother became seriously involved and began signing Communication Sheets and returning phone calls.

Eventually, Tom and Anne began to get along very well together. Tom became quite respectful, even to the point of reminding other students to show respect to their teacher.

Tom remained one of the toughest kids in school, which made a subsequent incident with Ted all the more frightening.

If Tom could be frightened by something or someone, it had to be serious. And it was.

It was Ted.

Ted had been at South Simcoe barely a month, but we already knew he would be a handful; Ted brought a history of violence with him and, as a matter of fact, had been arrested and charged with assault. We also knew that Ted's home life was somewhat chaotic. Ted was transferred to our school, after he moved out of his father's home and into a home shared by his mother and new stepfather.

Ted was tall for his age, with long dark hair and narrow eyes that seemed always to be filled with suspicion, and even the way Ted walked seemed to be designed to intimidate others. Ted dressed in heavy, oversized flannel shirts, jeans and work boots; he looked more ready for work than school.

One day, just before afternoon classes began, Tom arrived at my office door, clearly frightened. This in itself was disturbing; nothing seemed to scare Tom, or so he wanted everyone to believe. But Ted had threatened Tom with a knife during the lunch hour, a threat serious enough for Tom to report it. Sending Tom back to his class, I called Ted to my office and invited him to sit. I then quietly asked my secretary to call Ted's home and request his parents to come to the school.

Ted was sprawled across the chair, his entire body a sneer.

"You're new here, Ted," I began, "and we haven't had time to get to know each other yet." I seated myself across from him.

"I have a problem that I need you to help me with."

No response.

"Is it true you have a knife?" I asked. "There are reports that you have brought a knife to school."

Ted mumbled that he didn't have a knife.

I waited a few minutes. "Are you sure?" I asked.

"Maybe I have a knife," he said with a slight smile. "Maybe it's in my locker and maybe it's in my pocket."

"I want to know if you have a knife and where it is, Ted," I said. "You are not allowed to have a knife in the school. Besides, I hear that you have been threatening some of the students with it. That is simply unacceptable. I want you to tell me where the knife is."

The smile became a snicker. "Maybe it's in my locker," he said. His hands were in his pockets. "Or maybe it's right here in my hand."

"Ted," I said firmly, "you can give the knife to me now or you can give it to the police."

He withdrew from his pocket one of the ugliest, most fearsome knives I had ever seen, holding it not like he was about to hand it to me but as though he was prepared to use it as a weapon. When I finally took my eyes from the knife, I saw Ted staring at me in the strange hooded way he had, his mouth set in an expression somewhere between anger and determination.

Too late, I realized that I was out of my depth; I should have waited for the police to handle the matter, instead of demanding the knife from him myself. In one quick motion, I knew, Ted could thrust the blade into my body from where he sat.

I made a quick decision and called out to Joan. "Joan, can you please call my friend," I said. That was her cue to call the police. Then I turned back to Ted.

"That's some knife," I said, trying to keep my voice calm.

"Yeah," he answered in a voice that sounded like it belonged to someone ten years older. "It's to kill anybody who bothers me," he said. "And I'm keeping it." Then he slowly curled into his chair, one hand still pointing the knife in my direction, the other hand a clenched fist, the knuckles white. His eyes began darting here and there, and his body continued to fold into itself, like a coiled spring under constant tension.

OK, I said to myself, this is not just a case of childish bravado on his part. Ted is already facing two criminal charges, and he could easily overpower you if he chose to.

I had no way of handling the situation except through my words, and I continued speaking, keeping my voice low and my words gentle. I assured Ted that I would not try to take the knife away from him.

At that moment, Ted's stepfather arrived—a tall, casually dressed man who also, thank goodness, happened to be an ex-police officer. He took in the situation at a glance but made no comment as he sat down on the other side of the boy. He and I introduced ourselves as though everything were normal, and I explained that Ted did not want to give up his knife. Meanwhile,

Ted remained curled in the same position, the knife still clutched in his hand, with a new hint of fear in his eyes.

"I asked Ted to give me the knife," I said to his stepfather. "Since you're here now, perhaps you can explain the problem to Ted. Ted says that he needs it for protection, but it's against the rules to have a knife in school."

Thankfully, Ted's stepfather kept his voice as low and controlled as my own. "Ted," he said, "hand me the knife. You've heard Mrs. Dean say that you're not supposed to have it at school. You've already said you don't intend to use it on anyone. So why not give me the knife?"

Ted's response was to curl even tighter into his coiled-spring posture. I was afraid things might actually become worse, until the stepfather added, "You won't be in any more trouble if you give me the knife." He turned to me. "Is that right, Mrs. Dean?"

I assured him he was correct, adding that all we wanted right now was the knife. "Perhaps Ted wasn't aware of the rule against bringing knives to school," I added. "If so, I'll take his word for it."

The tension slowly began to ease. The stepfather continued speaking in a calm, soothing voice until Ted finally handed the knife over to him.

I breathed a long sigh of relief, and the stepfather suggested that he and Ted should go home and have a serious talk together. By that time, the police had arrived to take over the situation.

The police took over from there. Ted needed more than our

school discipline. He needed the kind of specialized help we were unable to provide, and we had to accept the frustrating fact that we could never solve all the problems we encountered at our school, no matter how much we wanted to.

In some ways, Ted was fortunate, I suppose. His stepfather not only cared about him but was a sensible and caring man, with the training and experience to deal with Ted in a calm, compassionate manner. It is ironic that other students, who were more likeable and promising than Ted, often had to cope with parents who didn't have those skills. What's more, these same students often became protective of their parents to a surprising degree, as though they were saying, "I know they have their faults, but they are my parents and I love them anyway." The bond between parent and child is a powerful one.

Nothing illustrated this better than my experience with nine-year-old Bobby, during one of our periodic attacks of head lice. This, by the way, is not strictly an inner-city school phenomenon. Head lice infestations in students can, and do, occur in the most respectable of suburban schools.

In any case, at this point in time, district policy dictated that students with lice were excluded from school, and of course we didn't want that. After all, we were encouraging students to attend school regularly and on time. Parents of students with head lice were asked to treat the problem with special shampoo, and to remove the eggs by combing the child's hair with a special comb, before sending him or her back to school. Some students returned without the necessary treatment. When we looked into it, many parents said they lacked the money to purchase the shampoo and comb. We arranged to purchase some, at wholesale cost, from the neighboring Kmart store, and we made these available to them.

In addition to asking parents to perform regular checks at home, we followed the practice of many other schools and began to inspect for lice each term. This angered some parents enough that they phoned the school to complain, stating their children were clean and well groomed, and we had no right to inspect their hair. We discussed this at a Parent Rap session, explaining that having head lice was not a sign of uncleanliness, just an unfortunate fact of life. Gradually, we won all the parents over by inviting those who protested most vigorously, to volunteer their assistance during scheduled head lice inspections. Soon the inspections became another accepted part of our routine at South Simcoe, and another demonstration of the importance of parental involvement in decisions such as this.

Bobby was among the students sent home for this treatment. He returned with lice still literally crawling through his hair. At first, he assured us that his mother had performed the treatment. Later, he admitted that he had lied. Once again, we sent the boy home, this time with some shampoo and a comb to be used on his hair. We also called his mother to explain that we could not admit her son back into the classroom until the lice were treated.

Bobby was back at school the following day. Unfortunately, so were the lice.

We repeated the procedure of handing Bobby the shampoo, calling his mother and informing her of the need to treat Bobby's hair before he could be readmitted to class. She gave her assurance, Bobby went home and he returned the next day with his hair as badly infested as ever.

I could not understand what was happening. Bobby knew the rules, and his mother acknowledged the need, yet nothing was being done to treat the problem. Just to compound my confusion, Bobby's younger sister, Jennifer, who naturally shared the same lice problem, had returned with her hair shampooed, combed out and shiny from the very first day. How could one sibling's problem have been solved and another's ignored?

I called Bobby into my office, determined to get to the bottom of the mystery. After several gentle questions from me, Bobby began to cry. I asked him what was wrong.

Through his sobs, he explained that his mother was often drunk when he asked her to shampoo his hair. "She doesn't like to do it," he said. "She just yanks at my hair and hurts me, and then she gives up." This was coming from one of the sweetest, most adorable and conscientious students in the school, and I felt my heart break a little.

"Wait a moment," I said as he calmed down. "What about your sister Jennie? Her hair was done right the first time. Didn't your mother wash Jennie's hair?"

"No," Bobby said, shaking his head. "I did."

You might almost expect a child like this to grow resentful of his mother, angry that she could not fulfill this simple task for her son. But Bobby did not. During the session in my office, Bobby admitted that he helped plan and prepare the family meals, sounding more like a concerned father and husband than a nine-year-old boy. Over and over, he tried to convince me that his mother was wonderful in many ways, except that she had a drinking problem. "When she's drinking," he said, "she just can't do some things for us, and I don't know how to do them by myself." In spite of it all, Bobby still loved his mother. I had to understand that, and in a small way, I did.

"Listen," I said. "What if we made arrangements to help you here at school? Do you think your mother would mind?"

Bobby thought it would be fine with her, so we did. A few days later, Jacki asked if I had noticed Bobby's hair.

"Don't tell me he has lice again," I said.

It wasn't lice. Bobby's hair was falling out. He already had a bald spot. An examination by a public health nurse indicated that Bobby was losing his hair, probably as a result of stress. Was it based on his home life?

One morning, Bobby's five-year-old sister arrived at school looking forlorn and wearing a heavy parka with the hood covering her head. Inside the school, she refused to remove the parka or even lower the hood. When her teacher finally persuaded her to, she discovered that her hair had been shaved off. Her mother's boyfriend and one of his buddies, hearing about the head lice problem suffered by the students, decided to shave the little girl's hair off. She was now completely bald and embarrassed. We, of course, were furious. I had no choice but to report the situation to the Children's Aid Society, who had been monitoring the family for some time, and they began arranging to place Bobby and his sister with a foster family.

Bobby was devastated. When he discovered the news, he came running to me, convinced that I was responsible for breaking up his family. In a way I was, I suppose, and I felt as though I had betrayed a confidence with him.

"We all have a duty," I tried to explain, "and my duty is to make sure all the students in the school are cared for." His mother loved him, I was certain; but at the moment, she was unable to provide all the care Bobby and his sister needed. Until she could provide it, Bobby and Jennifer needed help. "There is something else," I added. "The law tells us that we have to report things like this to the right people, who will find some way to help. If we don't do it, we would be breaking the law."

I think the idea of a school principal being in trouble with the law impressed Bobby, because he nodded glumly and said he understood. But he still wasn't happy. Neither, of course, were we.

Bobby and Jennie were assigned to a foster family in what seemed to be an ideal situation. They lived in a large, comfortable farmhouse with plenty to eat, animals to feed and care for and adults who treated them with love and respect. But the parental bond is strong, so strong that both children constantly mourned the separation from their mother. And their mother, when she was sober, also grieved for them, calling them on the telephone and crying together with her children.

After a year, Bobby's mother had improved her situation enough to win him and Jennie back to her home. Her drinking problem, she promised, was under control, and the children would be enrolled in South Simcoe once again. Soon after Bobby and Jennie returned to school, looking healthier and happier than I had ever seen them, I met with their mother in my office.

My biggest fear, of course, was that the children would find themselves in the same intolerable situation as before, and I suppose my concern was visible to the mother. "I know what you're thinking," she said. "You're thinking I won't take care of them the way I'm supposed to. Everybody is thinking that way. But they don't understand how much I missed those kids. I missed them a lot, and I'm trying my best to be a good mother."

I grew to like this woman. She was brusque and a little rough around the edges, but so were many other people. The most important thing, I kept telling myself, was that she loved her children, and they undoubtedly loved her, regardless of her failings. They were all going to try to make things better, and who was I to judge?

But I began to suspect that the mother was sliding back into her old ways. There was nothing specific, just the feeling that the children were enduring the same old problems at home, but with a difference.

In the past, Bobby had confided in us, and we had assured him that we were there, we understood and cared. Now he was secretive about his home life, afraid that once again the Children's Aid Society would become involved, and the family would be separated if the truth about their lives was revealed. In spite of her faults, the children preferred to be with their mother in their small house rather than on a large farm among caring strangers. Our attempt to improve their situation had cost us the children's trust and confidence.

Time and again, during those years at South Simcoe, we discovered the enormity of the problems faced by many of our students. As adults, we learn to cope with these complications, and most of us have the ability to address them in one way or another.

Children lack both the ability and the power to change their environment in a similar manner. They remain at the mercy of adult decisions, made in adult situations, and they are expected to accept them, often paying a high price in happiness and emotional stability. Nothing demonstrated this to us with greater impact or poignancy than Stephanie's rebellion, just prior to Christmas.

Stephanie had been transferred from a suburban Toronto school, into our grade eight class, in late October. She always dressed in expensive clothes, which made her conspicuous among the other students. During her first weeks with us, she appeared quiet and withdrawn but otherwise co-operative.

One day in mid-December, I entered my office to find Stephanie, visibly angry and sullen. All the students knew that my office was a refuge—one of our "safe places"—where they could go to cool off when their anger and frustration became too much to handle. Stephanie, I learned, had exploded in an outburst of anger, and directed her rage at her teacher, Doug. This surprised me, because Doug was noted for his patience and gentle manner. The cause of her outburst? A Christmas decorating activity, something the students usually looked forward to. Stephanie, however, called the work stupid and flatly refused to do it.

When Stephanie refused to discuss the situation with me, I busied myself with work to give her more time. Finally, I asked how she was doing.

"Not so good," she replied.

Stephanie seemed in no hurry to return to class, and I filed that away as I encouraged her to talk with me. Why, I asked, had she been so rude to Doug, who was a caring teacher trying to help her?

"He wants me to do some stupid Christmas thing for us to take home to our parents," she spat out. "And I don't want to do it. I don't want to have anything to do with Christmas, and I tried to tell him that, but he kept pushing and pushing."

I realized immediately that Stephanie's anger had nothing to do with the art activity. "You don't like Christmas?" I asked.

She hated it. "All you people keep talking about is Christmas, Christmas, Christmas. I'm sick of it. Don't you guys understand this will be the worst Christmas of my life?"

I told her no, I didn't understand. Then I came around from my desk and settled next to her. "Help me understand, Stephanie," I said.

It was like opening a door to a storehouse of anger, sadness and tragedy.

She began by asking if I knew how much it cost to celebrate Christmas. The gifts, the food, the decorations—you couldn't buy them without money, she reminded me. "I don't know what I'll even eat at Christmas," Stephanie said. "Maybe a sandwich, if I'm lucky. There'll be no presents, no tree, no turkey, nothing. My mother can't afford to do anything this year. Don't you realize what happened to me and my family?" she demanded. "We don't know what's going to happen to us, and you guys are running around the school singing and laughing and making decorations, and nobody knows what it's like in my home."

That's when the flood began. I put my arms around her while she sobbed and sobbed.

"You know what, Mrs. Dean?" Stephanie said between sobs. "I might be dead this Christmas. I can't take this anymore. I can't!"

Her words sent a chill through me. The threat of suicide from an adolescent cannot be ignored. At the very least, it is a cry for help.

"I'm puzzled," I said to her. "You're always so well dressed, and your mother has a job. Maybe you're not rich, but I'm still confused over your concern about Christmas and money.

Then I listened.

Stephanie explained that she was well dressed because the clothes she wore had been purchased when she lived in a comfortable area of Toronto. Back then, both of Stephanie's parents had professional careers, earning good salaries. The family owned two cars, lived well, took vacations, and life was stable and solidly middle-class, until her father lost his job. The father's search for work extended into weeks, and eventually months; the family was plunged into financial crisis. First, they lost their cars, then they lost their house, and finally, Stephanie's father lost hope. He abandoned the family, a broken man unable to cope. Stephanie heard he had become a street person. She neither knew nor seemed to care where he was.

Unable to afford housing in Toronto, Stephanie's mother had moved to the South Simcoe area of Oshawa, where rents were lower and from where she could commute to her job. But their financial situation remained desperate. There would be no Christmas tree, no Christmas feast and no Christmas gifts for Stephanie, as there had been in other years. There would be only sadness, and perhaps bewilderment that so many bad things could occur so quickly and with so little logic.

As Stephanie saw it, someone unseen and powerful,

probably a man, had made a decision that cost her father his job. Her father, in turn, unable to deal with all this, left. Now Doug, who in Stephanie's eyes was just another man with power, was practically haranguing her to be joyful, make decorations for her parents and get into the spirit of Christmas. Stephanie had no Christmas spirit; she simply had a reservoir of rage against people who had turned her world upside down, dumped her onto the cold ground and expected her to smile as though nothing had happened.

Stephanie's ordeal opened our eyes to similar problems facing other students in our school. We began to recognize and understand the unusual reaction of some students when facing Christmas, March break and summer vacation. Many students reacted by growing sullen, withdrawn and hostile.

We discussed this with our counsellors, Debbie and Teresa. Debbie was a psychologist and Teresa a social worker. Both explained that our children needed and loved stability in their lives, and any holiday break meant upheaval to them. They would lose a vital source of love and security when school was interrupted. Meanwhile, they were being encouraged to take part in what the school thought should be a joyous celebration, in total disregard of their inner pain. Was it any wonder that Stephanie finally exploded in anger and frustration?

We could not eliminate holidays and celebrations. We could and did, however, change the way we dealt with celebration times. We avoided raising false expectations of things that might not occur, and focused on demonstrating an understanding of the diversity in our community. We moved away from the material and social aspects of celebrations: gifts, families getting together, festive tables laden with food and goodies, and instead concentrated on opportunities for community and sharing. None of this solved the core problems of Stephanie and other students in similar positions, but we knew that it would lessen the ache.

Many of the students at South Simcoe were more mature and worldly-wise than other students their age I had encountered, in schools in more affluent and prosperous areas of the city. They had been dealing, for years, with social agencies, charitable organizations and, in many cases, the police as well, and they knew both the power and the limitations of these organizations. Yet, despite their problems at home, most students remained loyal to their parents and suspicious of outsiders. Combine that with remarkable maturity and deep sensitivity, and you encounter someone like Melanie.

Melanie was a twelve-year-old grade six student who carried herself with great poise, and was threatening to starve herself to death.

"That's what she has been telling the other students," one of the teachers confided in me.

"We know she's having problems at home, and she seems to have lost quite a bit of weight recently."

I agreed to have a chat with her.

Melanie entered my office as though walking into a theatre.

She chose a chair, sat down, folded her arms and stared straight ahead, looking for all the world like someone waiting for the movie to begin.

My efforts to engage her in conversation produced nothing more than monosyllabic answers, until she finally tilted her head and smiled at me knowingly. "I know why you have me here, Mrs. Dean," she said. "Some people have told you that I'm not eating, and you want to talk to me about it. Well, I don't want to talk about it. So you can stop beating around the bush. I'm used to dealing with people like you."

I interrupted her there, asking what she meant by "people like you."

"Counsellors," she said. "People who try to get me to talk so they can help me." She straightened her back and lifted her chin. "I can help myself."

She was very impressive, and almost intimidating—or as intimidating as a twelve-year-old can be while sitting in a principal's office. "You're quite right," I said. "I want to help you because I care about you and I'm concerned about you. We are all concerned about you. Now, tell me why you are not eating anymore."

"It's my body, Mrs. Dean," she said with total politeness. "I'm entitled not to eat if I don't want to eat."

I felt I was no longer chatting with a child but debating with an adept adult. It may be her own body, I agreed, but I was her principal and it was my job to look after her. Again, I asked her to explain why she was threatening to starve herself to death.

Still as polite as ever, she said it was none of my business.

It was time for me to become firm. "Look," I said. "You don't know me very well, and I don't know you very well. All you know about me is that I'm the principal in this school, and all I know about you is that you are not eating and you are threatening to harm yourself. I can't ignore that, because my job is to watch over the students in my care. I'm concerned about you, Melanie, and I want to help you. Why don't we at least get to know each other a little?"

This didn't work either. In fact, she told me she wanted to leave the office.

"I can't let you go," I said "without having some assurance from you."

Melanie threw me a knowing smile. "Sure," she said. "What do you want to hear?"

I told her I needed her to promise she would abandon her threat of starvation and resume eating. If she could not agree to that, she would leave me no choice but to call her mother. I might even have to call upon an agency for assistance.

This seemed to strike a nerve. "Why call my mother?" she said. "What about?"

I replied that her mother had a right to know what was happening.

"Sure, my mother would be worried," Melanie said. "But she has enough to worry about already, so don't you dare call her." She was angry, but I could detect a pleading tone in her voice as well.

"Then why can't you help us solve this situation yourself?" I said, exploiting an opening.

"If your mother is already having problems, why add more to her burden?"

It took some time, but Melanie began at last to discuss her feelings. She was not just trying to lose weight, she explained. She was not anorexic. But she was worried. What about? "Everything, just everything." School didn't interest her, and life didn't interest her. Then she said in a chilling and serious voice, "I just want to die."

I had heard children say this before, but in fits of temper, anger or dramatic despair. Hearing this intelligent and composed girl say it as calmly as if she were asking to borrow a pencil, was alarming. Thankfully, she knew the impact of the words as well, because she began quietly to sob. This was almost as painful as her words, but it also marked a breakthrough. Little by little, Melanie began to relax with me. I was careful not to say much; Melanie's words were more important than my own, although I told her several times that everyone at the school cared about her and was worried about her.

"You don't have to handle this all by yourself," I assured her at one point.

"Sure," she said with a hint of sarcasm. "There are lots of do-gooders around who want to help. Do you know what their way of helping is? They'll take me away from my mother. They've done it before, and all it does is make me and my mother cry. We cry and cry, and the people think they're helping us."

Melanie's story was familiar—so familiar that it was almost predictable. Her mother was an alcoholic, living with an abusive man. Someone had advised Melanie to call the Children's Aid Society for help if things ever became intolerable at home, and so she had. The result was removal from her home environment. "They took me away from my mother," Melanie recalled through flowing tears. "They left her alone with that guy and put me in a foster home with a bunch of crappy people who sat around and smoked and drank all day. *And I'm supposed to be helped by this?*"

I knew the Children's Aid Society had dwindling resources at their disposal, but I knew that even though they were understaffed, they always acted in the best interests of the children.

"I'll tell you right now," Melanie went on, "if you call my mother or the Children's Aid Society, or anybody, and tell them I said those things just now, I'll lie. I'll say I never told you those things, and you know what? My mother will back me up."

"But you also told me things were terrible at home," I reminded her.

"Sure they are!" she agreed. *"But why should I leave?* I want him to leave, but my mother is not strong enough to kick him out and...and she loves him."

She made a good point, identifying a serious issue in society: a defenseless woman invites a seemingly caring man into her life, and he becomes abusive. She is unable to make him leave for one reason or another, and when the authorities intervene, the child is usually removed from the situation, making the two innocent parties miserable. In response, Melanie had appointed herself her mother's protector.

When Melanie calmed down somewhat, she began negotiating like an adult. "I'll make you a promise that I'll eat tonight," she said, "if you promise not to call my mother."

I agreed, but not without some conditions. "The trouble is," I pointed out, somewhat appalled to discover myself bargaining with a twelve year old, "you'll know if I kept my promise, but I'll never know if you kept yours. I have to trust you to keep your word. If you say you'll eat dinner this evening, I'll count on you to be truthful."

Her reply was typically direct—and convincing, thank goodness. "I wouldn't say so if I wasn't going to do it," she said. "I don't need your approval."

Melanie was not, I realized, being disrespectful to me. She was simply determined to do things her way.

I don't know for certain if she kept her promise to me that evening, but I know that she abandoned talk of starving herself to death. When we passed in the halls, I would smile and ask if she had eaten that day. Sometimes she would answer, and sometimes she would simply smile warmly back at me, which was answer enough.

Melanie's attitude reminded us that social welfare agencies alone were not the answer to the problems of our students. For one thing, their finances and staff always seem stretched to the limit. Just as problematic, however, is the "one size fits all" approach that many agencies are forced to take due to heavy caseloads. We needed to find a method that acknowledged the unique needs and personalities of our students.

Finding effective answers to this enormous problem involved more from the participants than just the presence of parents, schools and social agencies. It needed a community-wide effort, and we were slowly demonstrating this fact in the South Simcoe neighborhood.

Bobby, Melanie and the rest were not statistics. They were bright, innocent children who did not seek the situation they encountered day after day, and could not alter it except by employing drastic measures. You could not solve their problems by tossing a few pennies in their direction and mumbling a few promises. They needed a totally different approach, an approach that focused on their strengths, built on them and helped them to become resilient. An approach that showed them who they were and who they were capable of becoming. They also needed to be supported and nurtured by respectful, caring and loving adults.

You could see it in their eyes.

There are many theories worth considering when dealing with social problems and their impact on children. But as Bobby and Melanie and many others proved, theory alone is simply not enough. It certainly wasn't enough for Barbara, a bright grade eight student who was moody and lethargic but, interestingly enough, always neatly dressed and well groomed.

Barbara often arrived late for school, without having completed her homework. Many days, she didn't arrive at all. She seemed not to care about school, appeared to be steadily losing weight and denied the existence of any problems at home. This, of course, was not true. Barbara had many problems at home, and she simply refused to acknowledge them out of shame or out of fear that, like Melanie, she might be sent off to a foster home.

Foster families may be safe and comfortable, but they aren't home. As hard as they work and as dedicated as foster parents might be, our students preferred living with their biological parents.

It took time, but the total picture of Barbara's life eventually became clear to us in all its poignant detail.

Both of Barbara's parents had worked long hours in their struggle to raise six children, and when the parents separated, Barbara was saddled with responsibilities at home. Washing her clothes, as well as the clothes of her younger brothers, was Barbara's job. Some days, she was unable to complete her laundry work and was too ashamed to wear dirty clothes to school, so she simply stayed home. She also played more roles than being her brothers' laundress; in many ways, she was their nanny, often dressing and feeding them, as well as a housekeeper, responsible for sweeping floors and performing other cleaning duties.

As if that weren't enough, Barbara's mother took in boarders, and the tenants often entered her room when Barbara was at school, stealing her belongings and invading her privacy. One of the boarders, a man in his twenties, frequently made lewd suggestions to her. With no lock on her door, she slept fitfully, afraid that he might enter her room at night.

Being frightened and overworked was just the beginning of Barbara's trials. Her chores at home left her no time to socialize with friends at school. She grew more isolated than ever, a condition made worse by her lingering pain over the breakup of her parents' marriage. She loved her father deeply, but saw him only two or three times a year, even though he remained in the city. Barbara's father favored her older sister, a preference he never attempted to conceal. To top it off, Barbara's sister had achieved an excellent academic record, a feat Barbara was made aware of through repeated comments such as, "Why can't you be as smart as your sister?" or "Your sister would have no problem doing that!"

It does not take a degree in social work to recognize that Barbara's situation needed more than a standard-issue dose of social assistance. Her already low sense of self-worth sank even lower, and she erected barriers to avoid suffering more pain from any source.

When the full measure of Barbara's situation became apparent, we all reached out to assist her. Often, our efforts were rejected. "I don't want your help," Barbara would say. "I'm too stupid. Leave me alone. Don't try to help me. I hate all of you." At other times, she might call us a bunch of "do-gooders" who only wanted to help her in order to make ourselves feel better. Then she might toss a book against the wall.

Once more: *You don't give up on children.* You don't write them off just because their actions are annoying and hostile. You get to the root of the problem and help them find a solution.

We refused to give up on Barbara. We began by assuring her that she could take all the time she needed to talk about her problems with Teresa, our social worker. Some days, she didn't need an opportunity to talk; she just needed a chance to cry, all alone, for a few minutes in a closed, quiet room before emerging, ready to face the balance of the day. We all supported Barbara through this period in her life, and she told us later that South Simcoe became more than a school to her; it became her safe refuge.

Things started to improve. Barbara became more trusting and increasingly confident. Her teacher discovered that she had exceptional problem-solving skills and liked math classes. She would offer to help younger students, who began to look up to her. This, along with our own words of thanks and encouragement, began to restore her self-respect and self-confidence. She needed that desperately. What she did not need were words of criticism about her lateness or poor attendance.

We had three years with Barbara before she moved on to high school. During that time, she made significant academic, social and emotional gains, and became more self-reliant. She regained a normal weight and eventually was selected as the valedictorian for her graduation class.

Barbara's problems had seemed overwhelming to her, a mountain of difficulties that she felt incapable of overcoming. Had we simply disciplined her for her late attendance and failure to complete her work assignments, we would have been adding to her burden and misery. Instead, we dug deeper and found the source of her problems, and offered her love, care, guidance and support. She leaned on us as she developed her inner strength and capabilities, and became more and more resilient. She was able to improve her life in ways she had once believed were impossible.

What are your current strategies to help students
prepare for holidays and celebrations, to ensure that
all students feel a sense of belonging?
If you would like to learn more about creating an
environment that honors diversity, please go to my website:
APublicSchoolMiracle.com.

Chapter 8

Creating Healthy, Caring and Respectful Relationships

Our guiding principle: *Everyone has the right to be respected and the responsibility to respect others,* was our compass, our point of reference for our focus on creating healthy, caring and respectful relationships. It was important for our students to feel socially, emotionally and intellectually safe; they also needed to learn how to create those relationships with others. *(Go to my website and download a full color, full size, print ready copy of The Hearts and Minds Guiding Principles.)*

Respectful relationships at South Simcoe was a two-way street; it was mutual—it applied to students and teachers alike. It defined the way we spoke and interacted with one other. Respect wasn't merely a "character trait" taught as part of a character education program; it was our foundation, who we were as individuals, as a school and as a community. Learning to demonstrate respect for self and others, and how this impacted on who we were being and becoming, was critical to our success.

The students, especially the teenagers, loved the idea that respect worked both ways, and that we would be as respectful to them as we expected them to be towards us. They understood that the right to be respected brought with it the responsibility to respect others, and they quickly grasped all the implications of this approach to understanding and dealing with their emotions.

Inspired by my grandmother's lesson, the growth and development of Respectful Relationships was graphically depicted on large charts around the school, as a series of concentric circles with respect for oneself at the center. Radiating from this were other circles, representing respect for others in the family, the classroom, the school and the local and global community.

We taught lessons on what it meant to go from principle to practice, what it looked like, sounded like and felt like to be a friend and have a healthy, caring and respectful relationship, and what it meant to be respected and respectful. We explained that respect for yourself influenced the things you put into your body, the way you dressed, walked, talked, prepared for school, conducted yourself, practiced self-regulation and dealt with others.

Respect for others, in your family, the classroom and the school, for example, meant having empathy for others—putting yourself "in their shoes"—to fully understand their feelings, listening to their points of view and being caring and compassionate when dealing with their feelings. It also meant responding with assistance when someone needed help, managing conflicts and solving problems peacefully and respectfully, instead of resorting to confrontation, aggression or violence.

Respect for others in the local community meant treating people as friends, as neighbors, as people we cared about and would treat in the way the students wished to be treated themselves. It meant respecting their property instead of vandalizing and shoplifting, two activities we were determined to eliminate.

Respect for others in the global community meant accepting and appreciating the fact that everyone is unique and worthy, so teasing and taunting someone for their differences was simply not acceptable. Instead, it was important to learn to respect and appreciate others and their differences. Respect for the environment and the world in which we live, went hand in hand with our learning, developing and growing.

Remember Melanie, the anorexic, worldly-wise girl who rejected help from social agencies? She grew more and more confident as an individual, strong in her beliefs and in her expectations for herself and others. By the time Melanie was in her last year at South Simcoe, she had had a stronger sense of herself and was much more confident. She never shied away from expressing her ideas.

One day, early in Melanie's first year at high school, I

received a telephone call from her new, and very agitated, principal. I knew this man well; most of our students attended his school after graduating from grade eight. He understood and supported our programs at South Simcoe, and was always courteous and amiable. This time he sounded perplexed at best.

"What the heck are you teaching your kids down there?" he said jokingly, but with a distinct edge to his voice.

It took me a moment to respond. "What do you mean?" I asked.

"I have one of your former students here in my office," he said, "who just told her teacher where to effing go. When the teacher sent her to my office, she called him every name in the book. I asked why she spoke like that to her teacher, and she said he wasn't being respectful to her. She said she's a human being and has the right to be respected by everybody. Where the heck did she get all that stuff?"

It was Melanie, of course. Fiery, mature, don't-mess-with-me, younger-than-she-appears Melanie. "We teach our students that they have the right to be respected," I assured him. "But we also teach them that with rights come responsibilities, and they have the responsibility to respect others as well. Obviously, she did not handle herself in a very respectful manner."

I asked to speak to Melanie, who came on the line sounding angry and upset. I told Melanie that we missed her at South Simcoe, and in my brightest, most cheerful voice, I asked how she was doing.

Melanie was having a bad day, which was hardly news after hearing the principal's comment. According to Melanie, she arrived in class that morning without completing her work. This wasn't the first time for Melanie, and the teacher responded angrily, refusing to accept her excuse. When he raised his voice, Melanie believed he was not showing her sufficient respect, and she raised her voice back at him. Unfortunately, she also added a few colorful and totally unnecessary words of her own. "I lost my temper," she agreed.

"How could you have handled this differently?" I asked.

"I know, I know," she mumbled. "But he wasn't respecting *me!*"

"You've backed your principal into a corner," I said. "You haven't left him many options. The bottom line is that you made a choice to swear at a teacher. I hope you understand there will be consequences for that. I'm asking you to accept them and learn from them. And please remember this: If someone is disrespectful to you and you stand up for yourself, it does not give you the right to do that in a disrespectful manner."

Melanie assured me she understood, and reluctantly agreed to apologize to both the teacher and the principal. She also promised to finish the assignment that had launched this whole incident, and to make amends—and do another one: suggesting ways to handle situations in which you do not feel you are being respected. She also promised to be respectful to her teacher in the future.

Melanie stopped by to visit me at South Simcoe a few days later, where we had a pleasant talk about high school, and how to deal with people who failed to respect us, and about life in general. She even spoke to the students about her own recent experience, and explained the importance of mutual respect and managing your anger to avoid such confrontations. When she finished, we hugged and wished each other good luck.

Unfortunately, Melanie needed more than luck. I discovered later that she dropped out of school in grade eleven, but she did return a year later as a part-time student. We made a great deal of progress with Melanie, but we didn't get as far as we would have liked to.

We didn't win with Jared either. We simply learned the limits of our ability to steer kids from disaster.

A tall student with an annoying swagger, Jared was transferred to our school from Newfoundland. He had attended twelve different schools by the time he landed at South Simcoe. We developed a good working relationship, he and I; we chatted together on several occasions, and whenever he became aggressive, I found I could diffuse the situation with a gentle reprimand.

Jared's constant relocation among schools had been disastrous for his education, among other things. Enrolled in grade seven late in the school year, he was unable to read even at the grade one level, even though he was almost fifteen years old. The future did not look promising. He began to hang out with older kids in the evenings and on weekends, many of whom had been charged with stealing cars and petty thievery. There were also rumors of drug dealing. Eventually, Jared ceased attending school completely, boasting to his friends that he was earning as much as a thousand dollars a week by selling narcotics. The police and the Children's Aid Services became involved, but it was virtually impossible to enforce any ruling designed to return Jared to school, even with the co-operation of his father.

Within a few months of leaving South Simcoe, we heard rumors that Jared was working on the streets of Toronto as a prostitute to support his drug habit. The news shocked us terribly. We had never had a student fall so far, so fast. Jared represented the limits of our ability to help our students. Even applying all we had learned by then, students like Jared had suffered so deeply for so long, that our best efforts were not enough.

Jared demonstrated that self-respect and self-reliance cannot be acquired overnight, even with a model like ours that was proving so effective with so many other students.

Would we have been able to help Jared had he come to us at a younger age? Sometimes so much intense rage builds inside a student, and there seems to be no way of releasing it.

Brenda was like that. Her moods ranged from sullen and morose to near out-of-control bedlam, and she had been in and out of various treatment programs over the years. At her most violent, Brenda would heave her desk and all its contents onto the floor before charging out of the classroom, and sometimes out of the school. Or sometimes instead of fleeing, she would lie down and scream at the top of her lungs, sharing her anger and agony with the entire school. At times like these, she sounded like a wounded animal in pain, and when the screams finally subsided, she would curl into a fetal position and sob uncontrollably like a lost baby.

Nothing in our training prepared us for this kind of behavior. It was doubly frustrating because her moods were totally unpredictable. "Maybe it has something to do with a full moon," one of the teachers suggested, half seriously. The moon had no effect on Brenda, but food did. We noticed that on days when she arrived at school without breakfast, she was more prone to losing control. Once we realized this, we made breakfast available to her, but Brenda rejected any direct effort to reach her. So we took an indirect approach.

Jacki recruited Brenda to assist in distributing milk and healthy snacks to other students in the school. In this way, she could help herself to food without feeling we had intruded into her life. Brenda felt good about helping others and ensuring they were well fed. Accepting this responsibility improved her sense of self-respect. Sometimes Jacki invited Brenda to the staff room to help wash dishes. Doing chores with Jacki seemed to calm her, and gave her an opportunity to talk to someone who cared.

We made progress. But the steps were tiny.

Once, a student burst into my office to announce he had found Brenda lying in the middle of the busy roadway in front of the school, causing a major traffic tie-up. He tried to persuade her to get up, but she swore at him and refused to move, claiming no one really loved or cared about her. Like Melanie, Stephanie and a few others, Brenda exhibited suicidal tendencies. In the midst of one of her outbursts, she would scream, "I want to die!" and the agony in her voice would be almost too much to bear. "I don't know why they put me on this planet," she might wail. "I don't want to live anymore. I just want to die."

With help from Debbie and Teresa, we learned how to handle Brenda's crises. She needed to hear that the feelings would pass and that things would get better. She depended on teachers to assure her of it, to the point where she found Jacki's number and began calling her at home during summer vacation, her voice sounding horribly alone, her words repeating her wish to die.

One evening, she called Jacki at home, crying over the telephone. In the background, Jacki could hear shouts of anger, and what sounded like someone thumping on a door or wall.

"What's that noise?" Jacki asked, and Brenda admitted she had locked her mother out of their apartment. Jacki suggested that she unlock the door and let her mother in. Brenda finally agreed, but not until she explained her actions to Jacki.

Her parents, Brenda complained, did not respect her. They

also, it became clear, failed to live up to Brenda's rules of behavior. As Brenda explained it, she had completed her housekeeping chores that morning in order to be permitted to attend a dance that night. But her mother broke her word and informed Brenda she could not attend the dance after all.

To a thirteen-year-old girl, this simple incident assumed massive proportions of unfairness and disaster. To Brenda, it represented yet more evidence of a corrupt world, one in which she no longer wanted to live.

Investigations by the police and the Children's Aid Society revealed extensive drug use in Brenda's home. Charges were laid, and Brenda was made a ward of the Children's Aid Society, placed in a foster home and transferred out of our area. It was Brenda who had reported her own parents to the police.

Lack of a decent breakfast intensified Brenda's rage through the day, and this was the case with many of our students. Steve Ramsanker had taught me to recognize the connection between a full stomach, emotional stability and learning, something he learned early in his career in Edmonton, where he introduced school breakfasts and nutritious lunches as a key element of his school's program.

Those two needs—for food and affection—may appear unrelated, but they are primary nevertheless. Those of us who have never experienced intense hunger in the midst of plenty, may have difficulty understanding such angry outbursts. Brenda's needs for food, affection and safety were not satisfied.

Instead of remaining a victim of her circumstances, Brenda felt that she deserved more respect, so she took matters into her own hands, stood up for herself and reported her parents.

It took a great deal of courage.

And then there was thirteen-year-old Brad.

Brad arrived in mid-term during my first year at South Simcoe, and he provided one of my earliest lessons in handling very violent children. During his first week with us, Brad was almost invisible, sitting quietly in class and taking part in few activities with other students. This wasn't unusual for new students. Many were being moved constantly from place to place at the insistence of one parent or another, and it often took them some time to build close relationships among their peers.

One day, Brad emerged from his shell. Or more correctly, a furious and violent adolescent appeared. Brad's anger exploded, triggered by another student's word or gesture, and he threw a chair against a school window, cursed his teacher and everyone around him and stormed out of the classroom and into the hall.

Alerted by his teacher, I went looking for Brad and encountered him in the hallway, walking back from the washroom towards class. His temper still raging, he was punching walls and kicking snow boots and other items down the hall ahead of him.

I said hello as he approached me.

"Leave me alone, you bitch!" he practically spat at me. I was taken aback.

It was time to show authority. "I beg your pardon," I said in my sternest principal's voice. "Do you know who I am? I'm the principal."

Brad was clearly unimpressed. "So what?" he snarled. "I don't care who you are. Just get out of my face, you stupid bitch!"

I was stunned. Over my years in education, I had endured insolence and rudeness from students now and then, but never with this much hot anger fueling the words. Brad was not going to respect me for my title alone, and short of suspension, no disciplinary action came to mind. I realized that I should not have confronted Brad while he was this angry, and knew that any response from me would only escalate the situation. So I turned on my heel and walked back to my office, leaving Brad standing there, looking for a fight.

Once in my office, I called Rodger, a colleague and mentor, and asked for his advice.

"It's nearly lunchtime," Rodger pointed out. "Why not get his lunch from his classroom, take it to your office, and let him know that when he wants lunch, he can get it from you there; when he comes to get it, tell him he cannot go back into the classroom until the two of you have a talk."

I collected his lunch and, on my way past Brad, I casually mentioned that I would have his lunch in my office, and that when it was time, he could come and get it.

It worked!

A few minutes after the lunch bell sounded, Brad was standing outside my office door, looking unsure about what to do and almost challenging anyone to approach him. Then he knocked cautiously and asked if he could have his lunch. I cheerfully pulled out a chair, handed him his lunch bag and invited him to sit down, as though nothing had happened.

"Let's eat our lunch together and chat," I said. My invitation surprised him; he had obviously been prepared for a tongue-lashing or at least some hint of immediate discipline. He sat down rather tentatively, and cautiously opened his lunch bag. I watched, horrified, as he withdrew nothing from the paper bag but a canned soft drink and a package of soda crackers.

"You know," I said casually, unwrapping the sandwich I had brought for my own lunch, "I had something to eat earlier this morning, and I won't be able to finish this sandwich. I hate to waste food. Can you help me out and take half for yourself?"

"Sure." Brad actually smiled at me. "I don't mind helping you out."

Does it make sense for a thirteen-year-old boy to become violent and aggressive as a result of hunger and malnutrition? Only a starving thirteen-year-old boy, feeling a little lost and dislocated, is qualified to answer that question with authority.

I had expected to review Brad's disrespectful behavior while we ate our lunch. But the look of gratitude on his face, and the way he wolfed down my sandwich and the apple I offered him, made me change my tactics. Instead of discussing respect and our behavioral agreements, we talked quietly and struck a deal. In addition to having a school breakfast, if his teacher agreed, the next time Brad felt himself growing angry, he could quietly walk out of the classroom and use one of the school's designated safe places to cool off.

"You have the right to be angry," I said. "But you don't have the right to use your anger to disrespect, hurt or insult other people or throw furniture." I added that there would also be consequences for the behavior he had displayed earlier.

Brad nodded his head in acceptance and agreement. Funny how a decent lunch can deactivate so much fury in a child. Or maybe it's not funny at all.

During the weeks following our encounter, I made a point of seeking out Brad, to offer him a smile and a word of encouragement, and to ask if I could see his work. Brad needed two things. He needed a decent, regular diet, and he needed to know that we cared about him. Are hunger for food and hunger for affection really so different from each other? Maybe not.

There was no immediate, total transformation in Brad. Other incidents of anger and rage popped up from time to time, but they became less violent and occurred less frequently.

When I began to examine Brad's life in more detail, the source of his rage and frustration became obvious and understandable. He often went entire days without having much to eat, and the sight of other children eating their lunches must have driven him mad.

He wasn't alone. Some children, caught shoplifting in stores in the mall across the street, were stealing cookies, potato chips, soft drinks and candies because they were truly hungry. Was it wrong? Of course it was. Was it understandable? I leave it to you.

In response to our students' need for food, we made sure that breakfast was always available for them at school. Then, with the assistance of nurses in our local Public Health Department, such wonderful people to work with, we set up our Healthy Snack initiative. We all learned about nutrition, what foods gave us energy and helped to avoid the mid-morning and afternoon slump, and what foods to avoid. We learned about reading food labels and looking for bargains so that we could get the best nutrition for our students.

Groups of students, working with their teacher, took the leadership role for planning, organizing and implementing this initiative They would do a daily school survey to determine who wanted a snack. Then they had to decide how much food was needed. If, for example, that day the snack was apples and cheese slices (a half of an apple was served to our younger students since they usually only ate a half; of course, they could always ask for more if they were still hungry), and seventeen students in a class wanted a snack, the students conducting the survey had to translate this into the number of whole apples they would need. This gave them an entirely new perspective on the concept of fractions and measurement, which of course tied neatly into their math studies.

Not only did this initiative help the organizing students to improve in math, it also helped to improve their self-confidence. All our students learned about the importance of paying attention to their health and well-being, and they became very conscious about the importance of a healthy lifestyle.

With a nudge from our school custodian Randy, the students took this initiative one step further and began measuring lunch litter. They would monitor students' and even teachers' lunches, to ensure that they were healthy and litter free. The practical benefit to the school, was identifying students who needed a daily snack, in a manner that did not single them out or embarrass them in any way.

At the start of the program, snacks were provided by staff members, who paid for the food out of their own pockets. I realized we couldn't continue to fund things in that manner, so we turned to our Kiwanis Club partners for help. They became involved, along with St. Vincent's Kitchen, and with their generosity, our students were soon munching on bagels, cheese and fruit, and drinking milk. Addressing the needs of hungry students became part of the school's everyday routine. Another risk factor—or in other words, impediment to learning—was addressed.

Why didn't our students receive decent meals at home? There were many reasons, most of them familiar and beyond resolution by the school alone. Many young mothers simply didn't know how to manage a household budget, or how to make inexpensive and nutritious meals. You could almost trace the income cycle of many families. At the beginning of each month, when funds were plentiful, the children arrived with full stomachs and ample lunches. As the month progressed, the lunches grew leaner, until, during the last few days before the monthly checks arrived, they would often bring no food at all.

Some parents, whose incomes were strained by numerous expenses, were taking money from the food budget to buy clothing for their children. When it came down to providing either full breakfasts and lunches or a warm winter coat and hat, they chose the latter. This was something we addressed with a clothing drive. Twice a year, we "sold" clean, used clothing collected from staff, family, friends, business partners and other sources, for ten cents or an item donated to the food bank. Students and parents alike could choose whatever they needed, and every garment that left the school was, to us, a potential meal fed to our students in their homes. This was neither a sale nor charity; it was simply a method of distributing clothing to those who needed it, and by charging ten cents, we did not offend anyone's dignity.

Using our guiding principle, *Everyone has the right to be respected and the responsibility to respect others,* as the foundation for the development of respectful relationships, was working; in fact, it was changing the mood of our entire school and community.

Our students were now understanding the social and emotional requirements of their roles as young leaders, and the kinds of relationships necessary in a vibrant and well-functioning team. With all that they had heard from our community partners, they were realizing that developing an inner strength, as well as a strong and grounded character, was fundamental to their success in life.

Little by little, students were taking charge of their own emotional state, and learning self-regulation. They were practicing how to remain focused on the positives in their lives and redirect the thoughts that triggered their negative emotions. This was no easy task. They were getting better at ignoring or walking away from challenging situations that, in the past, might have ignited an angry response.

It takes a great deal of time, effort and energy to develop the inner strength needed to control the impulse to hit or lash out in some other negative way, and to reach a stage where they were in control of their behavior, and all this came more easily to some than others. This social and emotional learning was a transformational process, and we carefully monitored and measured it just like we did for academics. Goals were set daily, and strategies were taught, practiced and analyzed. The data was then documented, discussed and graphed, and it became a part of the student's personal portfolio. This may sound like a long process, but it became routine. Students were taught to take ownership of the data and use it as a tool for growth and development.

In the more difficult cases, think sheets, daily anger logs and other tried and true school anger management strategies were used, and even the smallest progress was documented and celebrated at our school's monthly assemblies. This helped our students stay on course.

When we reviewed our progress and looked at the graphs depicting the dramatic decrease in vandalism, fighting, bullying and other forms of aggression, as well as the ones depicting the equally dramatic increase in respectful behavior, our senior students said to us that we should make "a bigger deal" of all of this and celebrate these accomplishments in a much bigger way. Naturally we agreed—why hadn't we thought of this before?

Our students suggested that we invite our entire community to celebrate with us; after all, they had helped us and had also been positively impacted by their respectful behavior. This would give the community an opportunity to show how much they also appreciated and cared about the students' efforts. They came up with the idea of a Respect Celebration lunch.

The mood of the entire school was one of excitement in the days leading up to what became the annual Respect Celebration lunch. The effect on one particular student stands out in my mind—twelve-year-old Roger arrived at South Simcoe late one spring from Toronto, bringing a long history of problem behavior with him.

Roger had been disruptive in class during his tenure at other schools. He mimicked teachers and students, was frequently absent for days on end and was considered a handful at the best of times—not the kind of student you want dropped into your classroom towards the end of the school year when things are running smoothly.

Regardless of his behavioral record, however, Roger quickly let us know how much he loved the way everyone behaved towards him at the school, and how much he was looking forward to enjoying his Respect Celebration lunch.

By this time, news of our Respect lunches had spread, and we were attracting more and more people who were volunteering to act as servers, including the Chief of the Durham Regional Police Services.

"I'm so excited about this lunch," Roger announced soon after arriving at school. We were frankly surprised at Roger's enthusiasm given his record. Roger was determined to enjoy this lunch before the year was over.

His actions seemed to prove it. Every few days, knowing Roger's troubled history, I would check with his teacher to ask how he was doing. Each time, the response was more than encouraging—it was positively effusive, not to mention a major surprise to everyone who knew of Roger's school history. "I can't believe it," his teacher exclaimed at one point. "If all my students were as well-behaved as Roger, my job would be such a breeze!"

Respectful relationships were now the norm, we knew, but

Roger's behavior was spectacular. Here was this really tough kid, who might have been expected to view this focus on respect rather cynically, changing his entire personality (as described in his school records). And he was a newcomer as well; our other students had taken more time to understand and appreciate the concept and practice of respectful relationships, but Roger grasped it immediately.

I called Roger into my office one day for a chat.

"I hear you cook a really good lunch," he said after settling himself in a chair.

"And I hear you've been an especially good student," I said. I told Roger I was very impressed with his work and behavior. I also promised that since he was progressing so well, I would personally cook his hamburger at the Respect Celebration lunch. The lunch, I added, would be served by officers from the Durham Regional Police, our business and community partners plus parents and teachers.

His face lit up with anticipation. "It's a deal," he said, and practically bolted from my office, anxious, I'm sure, to boast about my offer to the other students.

Over the next couple of weeks, Roger continued to be the model student, helping other students in class and playing games with them on the playground. He always wore a pleasant smile and told anyone who would listen, how much he enjoyed "this respect thing," as he put it. Then just two days before the Respect Celebration lunch was scheduled, Roger's teacher stopped me in the hall. "Something's wrong with Roger," she told me, looking distressed. "He's not the same. He's acting strangely this morning."

I asked her to send Roger to my office, and the boy who entered looked very different from the one who had been determined to sit down to a Respect Lunch. This Roger hung his head, spoke in a low voice and carried himself as though he were about to flee, strike out or simply break down and cry.

"Roger," I said when he was seated, staring at the floor, "what's wrong?"

"My father was hurt last night," he said. "They took him to the hospital."

"What happened?" I asked. "Tell me about it."

I expected to hear about a traffic accident or an industrial mishap, or perhaps a tumble off a ladder in his home. Instead, Roger blurted out, "He was hit with a machete, and they took him to the hospital. I don't know if he's OK or not."

I felt sick to my stomach. Suggesting I talk to his mother, I went to another telephone, called Roger's home, left my name and my reason for calling on the answering machine, and awaited a reply.

A woman who identified herself as Roger's mother called back a few minutes later. Instead of hearing the voice of a distressed parent, I found myself speaking with a woman who was annoyed with me and upset with her son. "Don't you people listen to the news?" she snapped. "Didn't you hear about the murder last night?" I told Roger the guy was dead, before he went to school this morning. Obviously, he wasn't listening."

I asked whom she meant by "the guy." Wasn't it Roger's father, her husband, who was killed?

"Naw," she said. "He was just a boarder who lived in the same house as us. He moved out a few weeks ago."

Only a year earlier, I might have judged this woman for her harshness, and for her apparent insensitivity towards her son's feelings. But my experience with South Simcoe families had taught me a lesson about jumping to conclusions, so I kept talking with her, letting her lead the conversation. Gradually, her voice became more emotional, and at one point, when I told her I understood her feelings, the line went quiet for several seconds. Then she began to cry. Whatever the relationship between her and the former boarder might have been, he apparently had been kind to Roger, taking the boy fishing and generally filling a father's role.

"If Roger doesn't know he's dead now," she said between sobs, "I can't tell him myself. Not right now. Not when I'm like this. Will you do it for me?" she pleaded. I called Roger back into my office and told him I had been speaking to his mother about his "dad."

"Is he OK?" Roger said.

"People who get hurt as badly as he did," I said, "don't always turn out OK."

He pondered that for a moment. "Is he dead?" he asked.

"Yes," I said. "He is." I waited for the news to sink in. "Do you know what this means?" I said finally.

"Sure," Roger said. "He's gone to heaven."

To encourage him to release his emotions, I began talking as two saddened individuals, not as a principal and student. "Roger," I said gently, "my father died recently, and it was a terrible loss to me."

We talked for a while, long enough for Roger to describe the things he and his "dad" had done together.

"When my father died," I said, "I couldn't concentrate for a while. So you tell me: what do you want to do this morning? Go back to class? Maybe work on the computer for a while? Or just stay here?"

Roger said he would like to work on the computer until lunch, which sounded like a fine choice to me.

Roger went home for lunch and did not return to school. Messages from me to his home, left on the answering machine, generated no response, and I feared we had lost him. We had grown so close in such a short time, Roger and I, and my heart ached at the pain and sadness I knew he was suffering. So I was surprised to see Roger appear on the day of our Respect Lunch. He remained subdued but talked easily with me when I told him how pleased we were to see him. "I am so pleased that you came Roger; you were looking forward to this lunch so much," I said.

"It wasn't just for the food," he admitted. "I wanted to be a part of the celebration and eat lunch with everybody, and I especially wanted to see if the policemen would really serve me."

Watching him during the meal, I realized how important Roger felt to be part of our special gathering, how much he needed the warmth and togetherness and how much he needed to belong. Yes, I cooked Roger's hamburger, exactly as he ordered it, and while smiling police officers and community partners served the other students, the Chief of Police served Roger his lunch.

Roger wanted to prove that he was good enough to be included, worthy of belonging, and he wanted the warm and loving feeling that comes from experiencing acceptance and love.

We never saw Roger again; he never returned for the last few days of school. Sometime during the following summer, he and his mother moved out of the South Simcoe area, as so many students did. I took comfort in the thought that we made a difference in Roger's life, if only for a short time, and hope that whatever trials he faces through the rest of his years, he will carry the warm memory of his time at South Simcoe and remember what it felt like to be respectful and respected.

We knew from the beginning that we needed to do much more than just correct and consequence our students' behavior. Since our goal was to make long-term behavioral change, we needed to go deeper, break the cycle of negative behavior and show them a different way of being and behaving. We had asked ourselves how many of our students really knew what it felt like to be respected and respectful. How could we expect them to maintain their self-respect and behave respectfully when, in most cases, they were the innocent targets of abuse, denial and neglect?

They had risen to the challenge and done themselves proud. Was it wise to honor, recognize and celebrate their successes? I have never doubted the wisdom of the idea.

During one of our Respect Celebration lunches, Staff Sergeant Bill Temple of the local police force talked to our students. Towering over the children in his service uniform and flashing a warm smile, he told them, "You must always try to respect yourself and other people because it's a good thing to do," he said. "Most times in life, no one will even notice what you do. You keep doing it because it's the right thing, and doing the right thing makes you feel good inside. That's what life is all about—feeling good about yourself, being strong inside and helping others to feel the same way."

I couldn't have said it better.

What techniques do you use to create
mutual respect in your school?
To learn more about co-creating respectful relationships
throughout your school, please go to my website:
APublicSchoolMiracle.com.

Chapter 9

Programs and Progress

Our focus on teaching our students to "be a friend," and create and maintain healthy, respectful and caring relationships, was working well and the level of enthusiasm was high, as evidenced by smiling faces everywhere. Academic and behavioral goals were being set and achieved; in fact, there was a significant change in the behavior of our students. It was wonderful!

Instead of school and classroom rules, we had created school and classroom *agreements*—standards of behavior and expectations, jointly established by students, teachers, parents and community members. Everyone understood and agreed upon what behavior was expected and what was not. We used our Congruency Consciousness Chart to detail what those expected behaviors looked like, sounded like and felt like. We placed these charts in classrooms and around the building. Our respectful relationships agreements, rather than rules, gave our students a voice, and since they felt included rather than imposed upon, over time, they began to take greater responsibility for managing their own behavior.

The teachers, relieved of much of the energy and attention usually dedicated to enforcing rules, discovered they had more time for teaching and sharing students' joy when they achieved their goals. They observed with pride their entire class progress in abilities and confidence.

Some problems remained however, in the schoolyard. We were still experiencing scattered incidents of fighting, bullying and other forms of aggression, and the more positive the environment inside the school, the more concerned we became about the continued school yard issues.

At that time, several studies suggested schoolyard violence and bullying was not only more prevalent than in the past, but was also growing more vicious and dangerous. A few years earlier, schoolyard fights were conducted with fists; then they began to involve knives and other weapons. The problem was not exclusive to South Simcoe, of course; similar incidents were happening elsewhere. What's causing all this terrible violence?

We learned from researchers that school yard violence was a complex problem, and there was no quick and easy solution. We decided as a school and community to continue our focus on intervening early, and putting strategies in place to prevent the development of patterns of this unwanted behavior. We learned that we had to help both the bullies and the children they chose as their targets, and that harsh consequences was not the answer. We reduced schoolyard violence dramatically by implementing a multi-faceted approach. We used our respectful relationships focus as the foundation, stuck to our non-negotiables and raised student awareness of the negative mental and emotional impact of their actions on others. We taught our students how to demonstrate self-respect, respect for others and how to create and maintain healthy, caring and respectful relationships—how to "be a friend." Just as this approach had worked for in-class behavior, it did for schoolyard behavior as well; it was not a muddle-headed theory.

It took a great deal of time, patience and the conscious and consistent use of language, but it worked. As our students respectfully defined and asserted themselves as individuals, they felt better about themselves; they seemed to develop an inner strength and resilience, and would neither harass others nor accept abuse themselves.

Parental and community support made a huge difference with this undertaking. We saw the greatest results with students whose parents agreed that the bullies must accept meaningful consequences for their actions, make amends to their victims and take ownership of the problem they created. Promoting respectful relationships in the home was a challenge, but their efforts made a big difference.

In tackling the issue of bullying and violence, we realized that it was so much more than a school and community problem. It was a societal issue, which needed to be addressed in homes and in workplaces as well.

It was so easy for us to make a difference with a student like Fred.

Fred was a grade eight student who took pleasure in taunting and teasing other students for his own amusement. He especially delighted in making offensive remarks to girls, ridiculing them until they burst into tears, then pretending he had done nothing wrong.

Fred's basic problem was his lack of connection; he was convinced nobody cared about him, and his actions seemed dedicated to proving this true. Each Monday, after spending the weekend with his mother, Fred appeared at school with a clean shirt, well-pressed trousers and freshly washed socks. From Monday to Friday, while he lived with his father, his cleanliness deteriorated. His clothing often reeked of cat urine, his hair was dirty and uncombed, and his socks would become so filthy that the fabric on the soles would harden like cardboard.

In the classroom, students avoided sitting next to Fred because of the foul odor that floated around him like a cloud.

Kim, Fred's teacher, and Susan, Kim's teaching assistant, addressed the situation by having a special session on hygiene during regular health class. No one needed it more than Fred, of course, and this was a creative way to address Fred's problem without singling him out from the rest of the students. During this hygiene class, they showed students a video on how to scrub their feet and trim their toenails with clippers.

During one class, Susan, a former hairdresser, made

arrangements for Fred's hair to be cut and styled for him. When he came back to class, the other students actually complimented Fred on his appearance, oohing and aahing over him. One girl actually told him that he was handsome.

This admittedly had nothing to do with the traditional "three Rs," but it made all these students feel good about themselves, and the impact of that single achievement was far-reaching. When Fred saw himself with his clean, well-groomed hair and new haircut, he blurted, "I look so good, I feel like a king!"

That was the end of Fred's taunting and teasing!

I was especially concerned about bullying and schoolyard fights because, as principal, teachers expected me to lay down the law with the students. That was fine with me, except that at the beginning, I found so much of my time being devoted to this single problem that I couldn't find sufficient time for dealing with curriculum matters.

We learned that the presence of an audience is a major incentive for bullies. When students watching an attack remain silent, they are in fact seen as supporting the bully's actions and giving him social status. Sometimes bullies who feel like *no*bodies, become convinced that they are now *some*bodies. Whether through silent assent or active support, bullies seem to need an audience to witness their behavior. Without one, their aggression loses much of it luster.

The good news? We built on our own success and developed specific and detailed Respectful Relationship Agreements for the school playground. This was supported by visits from our local police officers to explain and discuss the issue of bullying, as well as teach our students how to deal with bullies. All this reduced our bullying problem significantly.

Our students were now familiar with many police officers and did not feel threatened by their presence. They chatted with the students, talking about the dangers of gangs and the reasons behind bullying and fighting. They engaged students in role playing, demonstrating how bullies can be discouraged from their behavior, how to stand up to a bully and how to avoid becoming a bully's victim.

We learned that many students simply needed to understand what we meant by "bullying behavior," and how serious an issue it is. They seemed relieved to learn that violence should be regarded not as an inevitable experience in childhood, but as unacceptable behavior that needs to be understood and dealt with. Reporting bullying was helping, not tattling. Teresa and Debbie assisted us in developing and refining strategies to deal with bullying.

The link was clear: As students develop a deep sense of respect for themselves and others, bullying and fighting decrease. They recognize the importance of respecting themselves by standing up to bullies individually and as a group, or at the very least, turning their back on unacceptable behavior, denying the bully the audience that he or she craves, and seeking assistance. This takes both courage and character, but time and again it proves effective.

While we were teaching that bullying and fighting were unacceptable, we were also teaching students about the concept of interdependence and how we could all work together to achieve common goals. This became a major challenge, especially with students such as Tom when he and two other grade eight boys began bullying younger students on evenings and weekends. Tom and his buddies decided to create a neighborhood gang because, they believed, gangs earned "respect." They were basically good students who discovered how to flex their muscles and intimidate others, even while participating in school programs designed to counter these same activities.

I learned about Tom and his gang activities shortly before one of our Respect Celebration lunches. Tom's behavior at school was exemplary, and he was scheduled to be a helper at the upcoming Respect lunch, which created a dilemma. If he joined the group at the lunch, it would appear that we were overlooking his bullying behavior. If we excluded him, we would simply be pushing the problem out of the way and doing nothing to help him become more ethical and responsible. We would also be negating all his good behavior. Our students, I knew, had experienced too many broken promises in their young lives; they didn't need another one from their principal.

We compromised. Tom would have his Respect lunch and be served his meal as promised, but not with the other students.

He would eat it in my office, with me present.

And that's what we did. I served him, chatting and smiling, at a decorated table in my office. I explained to Tom that we could not celebrate respectful relationships with him sitting at the same table with the students he had bullied after school and on weekends.

His respectful behavior in school would be celebrated with me in my office. He listened quietly, finished his lunch in silence and asked if he could leave. When I asked if he had enjoyed his meal, he frowned and said, "Not really; it would have been a lot nicer if I had been with all the other students. No offence, Mrs. Dean, but it was no fun eating without them; I like being part of the group. I do understand why I could not." Tom missed sitting around the table, chatting and joking with his friends, teachers and community partners; he missed the family atmosphere created during our Respect Celebration lunches. Tom was disappointed, but he understood the reason behind our decision, and agreed that it was fair. More important, he learned a lesson about how one gained respect.

And as much as he wanted this from the other students, he realized that forming a gang and bullying younger students was not the best way to achieve it. Over the years, Tom did indeed gain respect and acceptance from his peers, but it was because he treated them with kindness and compassion and went out of his way to help them, both in and out of school.

One of the most aggressive and angry students we

encountered was Meredith, a bright grade seven girl with a beautiful smile and, at times, cold, hardened eyes. I don't recall encountering a child with both more promise and more rage than Meredith. She refused to be touched physically and was hard to reach emotionally. Just eleven years old, Meredith was already associating with much older children in the evenings and on weekends. Many of her friends already had arrest records for car theft and other crimes.

Over time, I watched in horror as Meredith's actions grew ever more intense. Her penchant for violence was shocking. On one occasion, Meredith fought with a girl so furiously that she broke the other girl's nose. Many of her physical attacks appeared totally spontaneous, without cause or provocation. Consequences meant nothing to Meredith. If she grew bored or angry in class, she would simply rise from her seat, walk out of the school and go home. When taken to court by the attendance counsellor, and warned by a judge, Meredith simply turned on her heel and left the courtroom in the middle of the warnings and admonishments.

Much of Meredith's life had been spent with various foster families, and she was receiving counselling from social agencies. While Meredith attended South Simcoe, she resided with a woman who we assumed was her mother. She wasn't. The woman was Meredith's grandmother. Although we had a few theories about the source of Meredith's rage, there was so much of her life that we didn't know anything about, and Meredith herself made it clear that she would not discuss the matter. Yet we grew determined to help Meredith if we could. It was impossible not to feel compassion for someone so young, with so much anger boiling within her.

The attack in which Meredith broke her opponent's nose, was a clear signal that our counselling efforts were not working. We could no longer risk injuries to other children. Home instruction was one possible approach, but social agencies familiar with Meredith's situation suggested it would be too dangerous to send a teacher to her home. What's more, Meredith's instantly negative reaction to the idea of staff entering her home made it even less practical. Looking for some guidance, I raised our predicament with officials at the board office, who suggested we use a library.

Give me a break, I said to myself. Where was I to find a library in this neighborhood?

A little later, I happened to be chatting about the problem with Louis, the new manager of the Kmart store directly across the street. I expected to receive nothing more from him than a nod of sympathy. Instead, Louis asked how often I would need space for Meredith's special instruction periods.

"About one hour, three days a week," I said.

"Why not use my office?" he suggested.

I was stunned, and deeply touched. Here was the manager of a major department store, who faced dozens of crises each day—including, unfortunately, the odd incident involving a South

Simcoe student—and still he was willing to relinquish his office space three times a week. But Louis wanted to help, and he believed both Meredith and South Simcoe were worth it. His suggestion demonstrated the depth of support we had managed to garner from our community partners, and Kim began escorting Meredith to his office for the special instruction Meredith needed.

Meredith's situation? You probably already guessed it. She was the victim of incest, and a bright and curious child who tried to balance her desire for a true childhood, with her inner shame and disgust, the only way she knew how—by lashing out at the world around her, especially anyone who threatened more pain and humiliation. My heart broke for her and, once again, I was reminded of the practical limitations imposed on me and the school system generally. We simply could not solve all the problems we faced.

Meredith responded well to one-on-one instruction from Kim. But just as we began feeling good about this small measure of progress, Meredith became pregnant, and she was still so young. She was removed from her environment by the Children's Aid Society. I wish we had had an opportunity to work with Meredith earlier; I am convinced we could have helped her avoid so much tragedy and pain.

We had our motto, *Together We Light the Way,* our beautiful symbol, our mascot Sharkie, and now we needed our school song. Sharon McLean worked with others, writing the words and melody, and soon we had our South Simcoe song. The song summed up, I believe, so much of the atmosphere we were trying to create, and the goals we had set for ourselves and the students:

We are the children who are looking to the future,
Sharing pride and singing our school song.
At South Simcoe School, we're learning every day
If Together We Light the Way, we will be strong.

We learn the skills that are going to shape our lives,
The sense of self that a good beginning gives.
And every day we're sharing with our teachers
and our friends
Who will help us all become the best we can.

We are the children who are looking to the future,
Sharing pride and singing our school song.
At South Simcoe School, we're learning every day
If Together We Light the Way, we will be strong.
If Together We Light the Way, we will be strong.
So Together Let's Light the Way, and we'll be strong!

We taught our school song to the students, and each class began singing it every morning, immediately following the national anthem. I would walk through the school, going from classroom to classroom, smiling and listening to the students and feeling so much gratitude for how far we had come. Only the grade eights were a little reluctant to sing, but that was understandable; by age thirteen or fourteen, certain kinds of public display can be awkward for many children.

Next, came our school chant, developed by Michelle:

At South Simcoe
We all know
We're the best
Yes! Yes! Yes!

At South Simcoe
We will, we will
Rock you!

Each time I recall our school song, I think of Meagan, and a host of emotions washes over me.

We were now holding regular school assemblies at the Legion Hall, to celebrate student successes. The behavior of our students during these assemblies was wonderful to see; they were so respectful. They entered and exited the hall quietly, they listened attentively, clapped and cheered appropriately and walked with visible pride to receive their honors. We ended each assembly by having the entire school sing the school song, and when we began this practice, we noted that our senior students still had difficulty overcoming their adolescent self-consciousness about singing.

Knowing that this was common at this age, we thought that it might help if they were led by their peers. When we asked for volunteers to lead the school in singing our song, among the small number who offered to perform the task was Meagan.

I was taken aback. Meagan was a thin waif of a girl with huge, sad, heart-breaking eyes ringed with dark circles; she had a lost look. Sweet and good-natured, Meagan had never shown any such initiative in the past, and standing at a microphone in front of hundreds of classmates, leading them in singing, is not customarily an ambition for shy and introverted students. But Meagan seemed determined, and how could we refuse her?

After the song leaders were introduced at the next assembly, Meagan seized the microphone in her tiny hand, positioned herself in the center of the group, and burst into song with a powerful bell-like voice, exhorting the other students to raise their voices with her. She sang with such power and confidence that we asked her to repeat the performance at subsequent assemblies. During one of them, David Onley and his CITY TV (a Toronto TV station) crew arrived to tape a three-part series on our school, and captured Meagan's exuberant performance.

Meagan's family background was in sharp contrast to her marvelous onstage persona. On the occasions when Meagan and I chatted, she spoke sadly of her treatment at home, and complained of her parents' excessive drug use. Like so many students we encountered at South Simcoe, Meagan was forced to deal with a wide gulf separating her life at school from her life at home. School was a place where she could count on being loved and cared for, a place where she received recognition and admiration for her talent. At home, little attention was paid to her needs as a young girl; no one seemed interested in her accomplishments, and the pain must have been very real and very deep to her.

Meagan was not dealing with her situation alone, and that both encouraged and frightened her. The Children's Aid Society had been aware of her home life for some time, and case workers were closely monitoring the situation. Knowing someone was watching and caring for her was encouraging to Meagan, but she also knew there was a possibility of being removed from her home environment, and this alarmed her.

Finally, a decision was made to remove Meagan from the house, and when the case worker arrived at the school to carry out the order, we knew that Meagan would not be happy to hear that she was being sent to a foster family. When she heard the news, Meagan rushed across the room and into my arms, crying uncontrollably. "I don't want to leave here; you are the only people who care about me!" she sobbed, begging Jacki or me to take her. "Why can't I stay with you? Why am I being sent away to some strange family?"

Jacki and I were on the verge of tears as we sat with Meagan while the case worker explained where she was going and why. Thankfully, Meagan was allowed to continue attending South Simcoe School, where she could count on our love and support. Thankfully, only one aspect of Meagan's life was being disrupted. Still, wrenching a child from her parents, no matter how necessary a move it may seem, is always agonizing to watch.

Once the pain of separation began to fade, the transformation in Meagan was gratifying. She arrived at school with clean, well-brushed hair, wearing attractive clothes, and she walked with more confidence than I had ever seen in her. Meagan missed her parents terribly, and she found the courage to report their drug use; but she agonized over her decision, even though she knew she had done the correct thing. She continued to lead the school in singing, but with a hint of sadness and regret in her large eyes, one that I suspected would remain there for a long time.

We wanted our students to return home at the end of each school day with a feeling of accomplishment, and look forward to returning the following day. Our goal achievement process helped this to happen. Every morning in every classroom (yes, even kindergarten), students set daily goals for themselves. At the end of the day, they reflected on their activities, checked if their goals had been achieved and selected a focus for the following day. By the emphasis on breaking goals down into small achievable steps, and accomplishing these steps, day after day, and then layering this series of small successes, each adding to the overall weight and impact of the others, the students began to become more confident about their abilities. Armed with this self-confidence, they began to take more academic risks. They were more willing to try something new, they asked many more questions and came up with more innovative solutions to problems.

As the years unfolded, we realized just how life-changing this process was. Reflecting on their day and asking themselves what worked well, where they had difficulty and why, what strategies helped them best and how they were going to continue to grow, develop and succeed, all gave them a sense of control over their daily lives and helped them to become strong and strategic learners. They were no longer daunted by failure; they simply picked themselves up, made their goal smaller, tried a different strategy and persevered until they achieved the desired results.

Many of our students still needed many things in their lives, and some of their needs were beyond the scope of our abilities to provide. Fortunately, self-awareness, self-respect and respect for others were among their most critical needs, and we were able to help them develop these. As they learned more about who they were being as individuals, and who they were capable of becoming, they developed inner and outer strength, they opened their hearts as well as their minds, and grew socially as well as emotionally. This gave them a core of confidence that made all of their academic achievements possible.

How do you align your thoughts, emotions and actions?
Are you ready to experience the joy of career fulfillment and
reduce job burnout? please go to my website:
APublicSchoolMiracle.com

Chapter 10

The Circle of Love

Something unique was happening at our school, a change so profound and positive that one of our community partners called it a revolution of the heart.

As the skeptics grew silent, others grew intrigued and supportive. We relished and embraced assistance from many sources, and in at least one instance, the help proved literally life-saving.

One of the organizations that offered to assist us was St. John's Ambulance. Our friend George, one of our most enthusiastic partners, arranged for his Kiwanis Club to fund a course on babysitting, conducted by St. John's Ambulance. The course would be taught in the school over the lunch hour.

We knew that many of our students would benefit from this training, since some of them, at ten years old or even younger, were being assigned to care for their younger brothers and sisters. We couldn't change the circumstances that led parents to place so much responsibility on the shoulders of such young children, but we could help our students acquire some basic safety skills. Thus they would be better prepared and more confident about handling this responsibility. And the bonus was that when they reached the legal age, they could also earn money by babysitting in the neighborhood, thus taking one more step to breaking the welfare cycle. Wouldn't that be worth pursuing?

Among the students who completed the course was Susan, fourteen years old and frequently called upon by her mother to babysit her four-year-old sister and seven-year-old brother. One evening, Susan and another grade eight student were babysitting the children when the seven-year-old refused to obey a request from his older sister. Susan, in an attempt to persuade him to see things her way, threatened to complain to their mother, noting that the mother would likely remove the boy's bike-riding privileges. In anger, the boy pulled a large kitchen knife from a drawer and hurled it in Susan's direction, missing her but striking his four-year-old sister in the leg.

Blood spattered everywhere, and as the little girl shrieked in pain and horror, the training Susan and her friend had received from St. John's Ambulance kicked in. They staunched the flow of blood, called 911, and rushed the child outside to meet the ambulance as it arrived.

At the hospital, surgeons praised Susan and her friend for acting so quickly. The Children's Aid Society persuaded Susan's mother to leave her job and accept mother's allowance, enabling her to care for her children and herself. Her son was enrolled in a special counselling program. Susan, of course, had proven the value and wisdom of the babysitting course, in a true life-or-death situation.

Education, I realized, could not end at the playground gate. Nor could the demands of life stop there. They both worked best when integrated—when social issues reached into the school, and education extended into the needs of home and family. Educational and social change went hand in hand.

The number of our community partners, our extended family, continued to grow, and best of all, their level of engagement with the students deepened. The students had also come to value and rely on them more and more. The Kiwanis Clubs, St John's Ambulance, mall merchants, members of the local police force and the Canadian Legion formed the early core of partners, and other organizations were added as the need arose.

It was serendipitous; it seemed as if as soon as we realized that we needed assistance in a particular area , someone would show up to meet that need. Within just a few years, South Simcoe Public School had become a symbol of innovation, positive school change, school and community partnerships and an influencer of social cohesion.

As we moved forward and deepened and strengthened our programs and initiatives, we made sure that they were all coordinated. Everything we did was integrated into the functioning of the school. Every program, every new routine or practice complemented and reinforced our vision and our guiding principles. Out of need, we had created a multifaceted infrastructure to support the curriculum and enhance student learning and achievement.

"It's a little like cooking three or four dishes on the same stove," I explained to someone. "The pots are all bubbling away, and every now and then you have to pay attention first to this one, then that one; you stir, you sample, you season and then everyone enjoys the food." That's what it was like managing all that we did at South Simcoe.

Our Celebrating Our Stars program was designed to honor and recognize our students and let them know how many of us were there to support them. Three "stars" from our main areas of concentration—academics, teamwork, social and emotional learning and leadership—provided a student with Triple-S recognition. The idea struck a responsive chord with the students, for a reason that, frankly, had never occurred to us.

"You know what I like about getting the stars and the Celebrating Our Stars ceremony?" a student said to me one day. "It's just for us. Report cards, they're for our parents; we already know how we've done. But at the Celebrating Our Stars ceremonies, all our community partners, all these important people, take the time to come and see us, celebrate with us and congratulate us, just for doing our schoolwork. This makes us feel really good. It shows how much they really care about us."

All students were honored and recognized in some way

during these ceremonies. There were no exclusions. We wanted them all to experience the feelings that come with the celebration of school success, and it would move us one step closer to achieving our goals.

In addition to a focus on academic achievement, our students were now aware of the need to focus on their mental health and well-being. Many had become more involved in sports and other school activities. They were conscious about their environmental footprint, and inspired by the service club members who worked with them, and they were encouraged to accept their civic responsibility and give back to their school and their community, through acts of service.

The idea of giving back reinforced yet another lesson learned at my grandmother's knee. She taught me that we all have something to give, and that giving always makes you feel good about yourself. "Even if we have nothing to share in terms of material things, our time and love are the greatest gifts we can offer," she said.

She told us that a wise man in India had said, "The greatest gift you can give is your time and your love." Years later, I discovered that the man she referred to was actually Rabindranath Tagore, who won the 1913 Nobel Prize for Literature, and his actual words were, "The greatest happiness in life is in service to mankind."

Our students welcomed the practice of giving their time. They loved having a larger role to play in their community, and they especially enjoyed the good feelings they got when they were kind to others.

Teachers and students alike worked together to determine different ways of giving back to the community. Someone pointed out that seniors in the area had difficulty walking to the store for a newspaper or other items. They lacked the mobility and energy of youth, which our students possessed in abundance, so this was quickly identified as one kind of service to be provided. Another service might be shovelling snow from the sidewalk for someone who lacked the ability to do it herself. A dozen other ideas were proposed: visit someone in the hospital or at a nursing home, take non-perishable items to the food bank, join a partner in the annual Terry Fox Run to raise money for cancer research, or simply walk through the neighborhood picking up garbage.

The acts of service were noted and, at the end of each term when report cards were issued, students were recognized with a citation on their report card. With just a little effort, every student could have a citation.

And they all did. All, that is, except Fred.

Fred had been gaining confidence and pride in himself as a result of the attention we paid to grooming. But he remained a grade eight student functioning intellectually at a grade one level, filled with enough anger and frustration that he refused to participate in the Celebrating Our Stars ceremonies. He was not interested, or so he said.

From time to time, Fred still insulted his teacher or threw a tantrum serious enough to send him to my office, where he would eventually mumble an apology and offer to make amends. During one of these sessions, I asked Fred why he refused to perform any acts of service.

"And I won't," Fred almost sneered. "I don't care about people, and I'm not doing nothin' to help nobody."

Fred seemed adamant, which was unfortunate in my view. By refusing to participate, he was alienating himself still further from the rest of the students.

Then something amazing happened. One day when Fred was walking down the hall towards his classroom, he passed a windowed door with a large smudge on the glass. He stopped, withdrew a tissue from his pocket and began wiping away the spot, as I stood watching, open-mouthed. I couldn't contain my excitement. "Fred!" I shouted. "You're doing something for the school! You're performing an act of service! That's terrific!"

Fred froze on the spot; he had certainly not intended to perform an act of service, and he wasn't sure what would happen next. I called Fred's teacher, Alvena, out of her classroom, and Kim Hutchinson came running down the hall from the other direction at the sound of my voice. "Look," I said to them, pointing at Fred. "He's cleaning the window in the door. He's performing an act of service for the school."

Fred grinned a little and resumed polishing the glass. Kim ran to her room and returned with a cleaning rag. "Here," she said, handing it to Fred, "this will work better than that old Kleenex," and Fred took it from her and kept polishing.

"You know," I said to Kim and Alvena as we stood back and watched him work, "Fred has definitely made a choice to perform an act of service for the school. What do you think?"

They agreed he had.

All right, it was pushing things a little, I suppose, since Fred so proudly refused to be of service to anyone in any way. We knew that he had not intended to perform an act of service for the school, but you know what? He stopped by to polish that particular pane of glass virtually every day for the rest of his time at South Simcoe.

Our first Celebrating Our Stars ceremony, similar to a graduation ceremony, was held in March 1993, my second year at the school, and no Academy Awards ceremony was orchestrated with more attention to detail and emotional impact. There was enough pomp and circumstance for a Buckingham Palace reception, and the students loved it. The formality, music, staging and speeches all made them walk a little taller and prouder, and to this day, Celebrating Our Stars ceremonies in schools implementing this program, maintain the same theme, elements and atmosphere.

As the students entered the Legion Hall in a procession for that first presentation, the theme music from *Chariots of Fire* played through the speakers of the sound system. At the beginning of the ceremony, two senior students mounted the stage to slowly unfurl our new banner displaying our logo and motto *Together We Light the Way*. The audience sat in hushed silence, and the children's faces shone with pride. Several invited guests, including our community partners and school custodians, were on hand to share in the celebration. I remember Sharon McLean reaching to squeeze my hand. "This is it, Sandra," she said. "We're really beginning to make a difference now." We both had tears in our eyes.

Meanwhile, the students were growing more and more enthralled with the ceremony. The names of the first few students to be honored, and the activities in which they had been involved, were read solemnly over the sound system. The audience applauded with enthusiasm as each student stepped up to the podium to receive his or her certificate.

The attention paid by the younger students, the staff and the invited guests was obviously important to the students, as were the descriptions of the actions behind their recognition. We took the time to describe each simple activity in detail—"Joey helped at Parent Rap sessions by babysitting. He also performed acts of service in the community by shovelling snow from his neighbor's walkway." Our students themselves were being honored and recognized as positive behavioral role models for their peers.

Why all the detailed explanations? It was one way of describing expected behaviors. Why the solemn formality? Well, it brought a sense of importance to the occasion, thus giving even greater recognition to the students' contributions; it made the students feel appreciated, not just for their actions but for who they were becoming as individuals, and it demonstrated how much we valued their growth and development as young citizens in their community.

Why the occasion itself? We had several reasons: It brought school, family and community together, to honor, recognize and celebrate the outstanding accomplishments of the children of the community, another step in our efforts to build cohesion and strength in the community. It also demonstrated that when schools and communities come together to nurture and support children as they learn and grow, great change can occur, but most of all, it was because we wanted to touch the hearts of our students, and have them experience the joy of school success. We knew that feeling would remain in their hearts forever.

At the end of the first ceremony, we revealed our piece de resistance. Kim Hutchinson, who was a great bargain hunter, had spent several days searching local costume houses for a shark outfit. It was not easy; a shark costume is not a common party outfit in our part of the world. She finally managed to find a costume so worn and moth-eaten that the rental company sold it to her for just a few dollars. With a little sewing, stitching and patching by our wonderful Pauline, it was made as good as new. As the ceremony was ending, we announced the arrival of a special guest: South Simcoe Public School's own mascot, Sharkie. Kim appeared dressed in the costume as wild cheers exploded from the students.

Everyone wanted to hug our mascot "Sharkie," and almost every student did. At that point, we knew without any doubt at all that our dreams of creating a sense of belonging, school pride and connection to their community for our students, were beginning to come true. These students, many of whom did not enjoy the opportunities available to students in other schools, were proud of their school, proud of their accomplishments and, most importantly, proud of themselves and beginning to stand in their power.

When it came to community involvement, the activity that seemed to produce the most enthusiastic response was our Circles of Love: Reading Together program. We had worked with our friend Phil Fernandez at Frontier College to develop this program, and we began by inviting children who were not yet attending school. We knew that if we could acclimatize them to the school and turn them on to books and reading, it would be an easier transition for them when it was time for them to formally attend school. We invited our community partners to read one-on-one to these children.

The simple act of reading to children yields many wonderful benefits. For the children, it helps to create a love of books and reading; for the grown-ups, it simply makes them feel good, and it also generates a bond between adults and children. Each time our community partners came to read to our students, both adults and students asked if they could do it again. Our own kindergarten students asked to be included, so they joined the group. These reading sessions generated such chemistry and such a special bonding that is difficult to describe. Perhaps Rob Pitfield, our partner from Scotiabank, put it best when he said, "It's like magic!"

Interestingly enough, many of the community partners who came to read to our students began to read to their own children at home. One partner, a senior executive in a multinational corporation, confessed that he thought reading stories aloud to his children ended when they learned to read for themselves. He changed his mind, however, and admitted that the experience of participating in our Circles of Love program prompted him to resume reading to his daughters, aged nine and twelve. He had been searching for ways to maintain a close relationship with his young girls, and since he travelled extensively as required by his work, found that he had less and less time with them. Choosing books from the library together, and reading from them to his girls on evenings when he was home, became a warm and special way of deepening and strengthening the connection between father and daughters.

Everyone we invited to participate in our Circles of Love— from parents and police officers, to the mayor, the president of General Motors of Canada, bankers, politicians, school board officials and the chief of police—responded with enthusiasm. Then our oldest students asked to be involved as well. They pointed out that reading to the younger students at school, would help them to learn how to read to their own children when they were parents. Imagine that! Our very own students proposing an idea that we knew would contribute to developing a more literate community.

We began with readings in the school library every two weeks, and it was such a delight to watch our students snuggle up to the partners, their eyes wide and shining, while they listened to the stories. It was especially dramatic when the person reading to them was a male business executive in a suit, or a policeman in full uniform; they didn't have many male role models in their lives since our community was filled with so many single mothers. It was wonderful for our boys to see men assuming a parenting role, taking time from their business or careers to read stories and chat with students. It showed them that men did see children as important, and it also gave them great role models to emulate. The presence of the men could never, of course, take the place of an absent father, or mitigate abuse from their mother's live-in boyfriend. But it was important nevertheless.

Among the male role models who proved especially popular with our students was one of the tallest uniformed police officers I had ever encountered. Colin Shaw stood well over six feet and arrived at the school in full regalia, including handcuffs, sidearm and billy club, and actually stretched himself full length on the floor to read aloud to the students.

In the beginning, they couldn't resist peppering him with questions about his weapon and his handcuffs, and if he had ever appeared on the TV show *Cops*. As time passed, however, they grew more relaxed around Colin. They loved to wear his hat, and the conversations they shared with him extended to include music, fashion, sports and movies—all the diversions important to children yet rarely discussed with adults, let alone a uniformed police officer. Eventually, the students didn't seem to notice the uniform at all.

Colin began visiting the school regularly to chat with students, often arriving in his police cruiser. Several months earlier, the sight of a police cruiser parked at the school signaled bad news to the students and their parents, who assumed someone was in trouble with the law. Now the sight of a cruiser produced little more than a shrug of the shoulders and the observation, "It's probably just the police reading to the children."

And it almost always was.

Later, our Circles of Love expanded beyond the school. We held several sessions at local shopping malls, where we invited students from other schools to join us to listen to stories read to them by the mayor and the chief of police. This became an annual event, and neither one of them ever missed a session. Even later, when our programs spread to schools across Canada, we were invited by the parliamentary spouses to hold sessions in the Senate Chambers at the House of Parliament in Ottawa. Colin was there too.

We welcomed surprise visitors to our Circles of Love

sessions, from all walks of life and from all sources. When Curt Tingley, one of our community partners, encountered cartoonist and author Ben Wicks at an airport lounge and described our program to him, Ben agreed to visit us. He read to the students and drew cartoons for them, often exaggerating his Cockney accent for comic effect.

We were grateful for all the involvement that was pledged to us, but I remember we were especially touched by the assistance we received from Jim, the owner of a small pizza parlour near the school. The young franchise owner was among the first to offer his help, and I was amazed that he was not only an enthusiastic supporter but that he even made time to spend with the students.

The pizza store was not a big money-maker for him; he was actually holding down two additional jobs, and he was certainly not a wealthy man. But he believed in our shared vision and the goals we were trying to achieve, and he wanted to give something back to the community. So he visited the school regularly to talk to the students about setting goals, making choices, staying in school and obtaining an education and the feeling of satisfaction that comes from a job well done. He certainly filled the role of the kind of dedicated neighborhood businessman we wanted our students exposed to.

Jim knew that many of our students could not afford to buy his pizza, so he helped to organize "Thursday pizza days," paring his profit to the bone so that our students could enjoy his pizza for lunch one day a week. He was such a wonderful role model for our students.

We were now in our third year and were so buoyed by our success in engaging our community and the student gains as a result, that we wanted to pay tribute to them and give them a great big "thank you." We wanted an impossible-to-ignore, in-your-face event that said to the community, *"Don't you just love us??!!"* and defied anyone to disagree. This event had to be done in the most active, vocal and visible way we could. And what, we asked, is more active, vocal and visible than a parade of students?

We started off the school year with our Community Parade. The first parade involved our students, led by school staff, walking through the neighborhood and leaving thank you notes for our community partners. The following year, everyone wanted to be involved, so our community partners, parents and even the business mascots were included.

The entire procession was led by Constable Colin Shaw in his police cruiser, followed by our very own Sharkie, students, the Swiss Chalet Chicken, the Kmart Cougar, Marty, the Shoppers Drug Mart Shutterbug, the Pizza Pizza Doughboy and a GM truck bringing up the rear. One way or another, often juggling her busy schedule, the mayor participated as well.

In order to keep school spirit high and reinforce a sense of connectedness and belonging to the school, we engaged in fun activities such as creating class names. Each class chose a name linked to our motto, *Together We Light the Way.* They came up with names like *The Grade Five Firecrackers, The Grade Four Flaming Eagles, The Grade Six Shooting Stars* and even *The Kindergarten Kilowatts.* I suspect this class had some input from their teacher, unless I seriously underestimated the awareness and vocabulary of our kindergarten students. The students then made class name banners, complete with their own decorative touches.

The students really enjoyed this type of activity and, on another, deeper level, it strengthened the connection of the students to the school and the community. Children who feel isolated, not connected, often become lost, and those who feel lost can drift towards problems—poor school work, delinquency and, in extreme cases, even suicide.

During our parade, each class carried their banner bearing their class name. The younger students wore colorful balloons tied to their wrists. Everyone sang the school song as they marched, guided by staff and parents. We stopped in front of each business place, where the students would repeat the South Simcoe Chant while waiting for the manager or owner to emerge, and then two students from each class would hand the proprietor a note thanking them for their support, and a clean-up certificate, promising to return within a few days to clean up around their place of business, as part of their community clean-up thank you.

The first stop was always the nearby Legion Hall, where the

students assembled in front of the building to be greeted by the manager and his staff. After saying thank you, the students would launch into the school chant, delivered in lusty voices with arms raised in the air, followed by laughter and applause. Then we would move on to greet the next community partner and repeat the process.

Our route was not a long one, because many of the little legs in grade one couldn't handle a major trek. The kindergarten classes rode in a school bus decorated with cat whiskers, provided by Laidlaw, another community partner.

New supporters were continuously popping up throughout the community. One day in June, I received a letter from Dr. Frank Gold, a local dentist who occupied an office in the mall across the street. Hearing of our progress at South Simcoe, Dr. Gold congratulated us on the program and expressed a desire to participate. Although we always welcomed new partners, we weren't certain of the potential role for a dentist in the program, and it was too late to accept his services for that school year anyway. In fact, we didn't even have time to reply to him before the onset of summer vacation.

During our parade in September, however, I got a rather mischievous idea. Instead of drafting a letter to Dr. Gold, thanking him for his offer of support, why not thank him in person?

We made a short detour to Dr. Gold's office, assembled outside his door and began chanting his name—"Doctor Gold!

Doctor Gold!"—over and over.

The sound of hundreds of voices shouting his name must have alarmed the poor doctor terribly, not to mention the bewildered patient seated in his dental chair. Dr. Gold appeared at the door wearing his white dentist's gown, holding a dental instrument in rubber-gloved hands and wearing an expression of confusion and concern. I quickly explained that we had appreciated his offer of assistance so much that we chose to express our thanks with a visit from the entire school. He broke into a smile while the students applauded and cheered him, and he then excused himself to scurry back inside to finish treating his anxious patient.

Dr. Gold became yet another active partner in the programs at South Simcoe, and eventually confessed that he had been thrilled by our impetuous visit.

Most schools launched each new school year with a Meet the Teacher event. By our third year, "Meet the Teacher" no longer seemed appropriate, because so many other individuals had now made a commitment to work with us and become a part of the teaching/learning process, including a large number of parents, business and community partners.

Instead of Meet the Teacher night, we held the South Simcoe Community Get-Together. We held it on the school grounds, following our parade, and it was like a large family picnic. The entire area was decorated with balloons and banners. We all dined on hot dogs and hamburgers, and drank iced tea and lemonade, provided by the Kiwanis Club and our friends at Swiss Chalet. Games, pony rides and jumping toys kept the students amused and burned off excess energy.

The community had come together to forge relationships around the common cause of educating our students, and the Get-Togethers served many purposes. They provided a gathering time for everyone involved in the cause, and they became an opportunity to begin the new school year by celebrating our past achievements, while setting the stage for new ones in the coming year. These gatherings created a sense of community and belonging that went beyond the occasion and carried forth those feelings over the course of the year.

By this time, even minor disasters were unable to spoil our success. For our first Community Get-Together, two teachers were assigned to light the barbecues and begin cooking hamburgers and hot dogs. The day was unusually windy, however, and neither teacher was able to get the barbecues lit.

Kim Hutchinson sprang into action. Seizing a cooler filled with raw hamburgers and sprinting across the street to the Swiss Chalet restaurant, she explained the situation to our friend Phil Lawson, and without a moment's hesitation, he said, "Leave it to me." We still don't know how he managed to cook so many hamburgers so quickly, in a kitchen equipped to broil chicken. As many patrons waited patiently for their broiled-chicken dinners, delayed by our hamburgers and hot dogs, Kim entertained them with stories of the accomplishments of South

Simcoe students, adding that the children were very hungry and waiting patiently for their meal. It worked; when Kim sprinted out the door with the cooked hamburgers, several diners actually applauded!

A few months later, when Swiss Chalet announced it would be adding hamburgers to its menu, we jokingly remarked that this minor revolution in corporate policy must have been launched during our Community Get-Together at South Simcoe.

One morning in early November, several students came running to me before classes began, obviously distressed. "There's a fire down the street!" they announced. "And it's in the house where some of our students live!" The blaze was a block away, and after confirming from the fire fighters that our students were safe and it would be unnecessary to evacuate the school, I investigated the circumstances. Three children, recently enrolled in the school, resided in the house. We discovered them, along with their distraught mother and a baby in diapers and wrapped with a thin blanket, seated in a van nearby. It happened to be a bitterly cold day, and we could either wait for one of the social agencies to arrive or take charge ourselves. Jacki and I put our heads together and decided to take charge.

We went out to the van, met the family, carried the baby inside and made the mother some hot tea. Then we rummaged through our "lost and found," and pulled out a warm blanket and oversized woolen socks for the baby. We calmed the family as much as we could. The parents needed to talk with fire authorities, arrange for new accommodations, find a kennel for the family dog and reassure concerned relatives. We told them to leave the children, including the baby, with us.

The student response was wonderful; they were all very concerned. The president of the Students' Council approached me and asked for permission to call a student leadership meeting to discuss how they could assist the family. Naturally I agreed, and watched with a lump in my throat while he and the rest of his team took charge. They outlined the family's plight and their immediate needs. "They have just had a real loss," the Students' Council president pointed out. "They are all frightened, especially the children, and don't know if anything is left at their house. They have nothing, not even clothes for the baby. So how can we help them?"

It seemed as if all the leadership skills they had been learning suddenly kicked in. They brainstormed ideas and came up with a plan. Many returned from lunch with food, clothing and, best of all, ideas. Someone pointed out that it wouldn't be fair for the older child, a girl, to miss classes because she needed to take care of the baby. "Let's take turns babysitting," another proposed, and they quickly established a schedule. The rest of the day passed quietly, with students continuously inquiring about the family's situation and, I realized, enjoying their role as a collective hero. Meanwhile, I felt as though I were about to burst with pride. The students had reacted immediately to the situation. They took the initiative, assumed leadership roles and accepted responsibility with the confidence of individuals twice their age.

As things turned out, Pam, the mother, was unable to return to retrieve the children until very late that evening. After everyone left, I remained at the school, playing the roles of principal, babysitter and fill-in mother. It seemed as if the three children were everywhere at once, keeping me busy changing diapers, preparing snacks, offering reassurances and tidying things up while they demonstrated their energy and curiosity. Ah, the life of a public school principal.

Not surprisingly, both parents became exceptionally strong school supporters. More gratifying to me, however, was the manner in which our wonderful students responded to that one-day crisis. Spontaneously and with love, they rose to the occasion and looked out for one another. They reached out in compassion to those in need, just as the community had responded to them.

Look what we've done, I reflected in the days following the fire. Together, the school and community had fostered changes that would have been unimaginable a few years earlier. At one point, the students of South Simcoe Public School had been considered the source of problems in the neighborhood. Now they were young leaders, confident, responsible, caring and loving individuals, who generated so much pride and affection in the hearts of all those who knew them.

Especially their principal.

*How do you increase student engagement
and desire for achievement?
If you would like to learn additional strategies to
encourage student achievement go to my website:
APublicSchoolMiracle.com.*

Chapter 11

From Worst to First

By the third year, we were well on our way, and word of our success began to spread beyond the neighborhood and the city of Oshawa. In the fall of 1994, I was surprised to receive a call from the Canadian Broadcasting Corporation, which was dedicating an episode of their award-winning *Man Alive* television series to the subject of resilient children. The network dispatched crews from Toronto to visit schools all across Canada in search of the most outstanding programs for building resilience in children. When they arrived in Edmonton to discuss the project with Steve Ramsanker, he was amazed to see them. "Why did you travel all this way," Steve asked them, "when you have a wonderful example right in your own backyard, in Oshawa?

For almost five weeks, we shared the school with TV cameras, lights, sound equipment and TV crew members, as they captured our daily routines and ventured into some students' homes to interview parents and children.

The show aired across Canada early in 1995, and within a day or two, I received a telephone call from Jennifer, an executive with General Motors of Canada. GM was looking for someone from outside the automotive industry to share their leadership success story at a marketing conference attended by managers from the company's Ontario zone. One condition, they asked, was that I avoid any kind of formal presentation—no notes, no charts, no overhead projection materials. "Just be prepared to field questions," Jennifer suggested.

I was concerned about my ability to make a presentation under those circumstances, but my nervousness quickly dissipated when the 150 GM managers rose to their feet and applauded as I entered the conference room. The time flew past quickly and easily. What's more, the audience seemed genuinely pleased with, and surprised at, the simplicity of my answers to their questions, and proved it with thunderous applause at the end.

Afterwards, Jennifer asked if they could do anything for me in return—a monetary contribution to the school, perhaps?

"It would be so easy for you to write a check," I replied. "But money is not the most valuable thing you can contribute. Our students need support from their community; they need mentors, and we need that for the long term. People like you and your colleagues, who work in such a large corporation and are so successful, need to visit our school, meet our students and spend time mentoring them."

My suggestion unleashed an outpouring of new support from the people in GM's Ontario zone. Jennifer McDonald, Barry Kuntz and their staff joined our Circles of Love, Reading Together Program, arriving regularly to read aloud to our younger students, and eventually participating in other programs as well.

Then something extraordinary happened. When Jennifer and Barry saw our programs in action, witnessed the students setting and achieving goals, and studied the affirmations displayed throughout the school, they asked if they could bring several Ontario-zone employees with them on their next visit to job shadow us. Fascinated by our achievements, they were especially interested in what was making us such a powerful team. They wanted to observe us in action, see firsthand how we shared leadership and unveil whatever "magic formula" we had managed to create, and apply it to their own work activities. We agreed, of course, and watched as our visitors grew intrigued by our methods of sharing leadership, goal achievement and community building, our focus on the creation of respectful and caring relationships, and our emphasis on always keeping a smile on our faces—staff and students alike.

They noted with interest our asset-based philosophy in action, the way we always began with a student's strengths, then moved to areas for growth and development, never talking about weakness and deficiencies. They marveled at our ability to achieve so much with so few material assets. They appreciated our refusal to focus on things we did not have, and our insistence on emphasizing the resources we did have instead.

They loved our "heart builders," our *Bouquet Board*, our *Respect Tree*, our charts and team rituals and so much more. Barry told me that they actually adopted many of our ideas and wove them into their GM training programs. When other GM zones grew aware of the lessons to be learned from South Simcoe, they invited me to speak to their groups as well. As a result, I travelled to British Columbia's beautiful Okanagan Valley, Calgary, Alberta, Prince Edward Island and Winnipeg, Manitoba. The warmth of the hospitality in Winnipeg countered the January weather, as did viewing the *Man Alive* documentary on a giant IMAX screen. At each location, when they asked me what I wanted from them in return for my speaking, I asked my audience to get involved with the students in the school nearest to them and mentor them in some way.

"All children need to know they are valued, and for students like the ones at South Simcoe, who may face more challenges in life, support from people like you can make all the difference," I said. "Work with me and make a difference!"

What an amazing development! South Simcoe Public School, located in the heart of Oshawa's inner city, was teaching important lessons to a division of one of the world's largest, most dynamic corporations. It put an entirely new spin on the idea of "community engagement."

Community support at its best is a two-way street, with each side taking turns at giving and receiving. We are proud that Barry, Tom and other members of their team at GM valued our school as a source of management and teamwork training ideas. And we were gratified when they and other GM employees helped us turn a potentially tragic Christmas into a joyous event one year.

It concerned Penny and her children. Penny, a single mother struggling valiantly to better herself and her children, had become a strong advocate for our programs at the school. A regular participant in Parent Rap sessions, Penny had moved out of the neighborhood in search of better living conditions, yet insisted on her children continuing to attend our school because of the relationships they had built. She and her family shared an apartment with a second family that included two teenaged boys.

With only mother's allowance as her income, Penny managed to set aside enough money each week so that, in mid-December, she was able to purchase some food, treats and a few gifts for her children to enjoy at Christmas. The holiday season meant a great deal to Penny, and she looked forward to seeing the smiles on the faces of her children on Christmas Day. They would open their gifts in the morning and share what would be for them a somewhat elaborate meal that evening.

But it was not to be. A week before Christmas, the other family's teenaged boys raided the freezer, sold or ate most of Penny's food and threw away whatever they had no use for. In addition, they stole the gifts Penny had wrapped and hidden for her children, selling them on the street for money to play video games.

Penny was devastated. Life, which had been hard for her for so many years, had turned cruelly unfair. No social assistance checks would arrive before Christmas. There would be no presents for her children, no modest feast and very little joy.

Jacki heard of Penny's situation and passed the news on to me. Could we do anything to help the family? It didn't look very promising. All our normal sources of assistance at Christmas had already donated to needy families; it was unfair to call them now, so close to the holiday. In quiet desperation, I called Tom at General Motors, and quickly explained the situation to him.

He recognized my description of Penny almost immediately. "Wasn't she in the *Man Alive* video?" he asked.

I told him she was indeed.

"A lot of people around here saw that broadcast and were moved by it," he said. "And some heard you speak here. I don't know what I can do on short notice, but I'll try my best."

What he did was virtually miraculous. When word spread throughout the GM zone offices where I had spoken, we became almost inundated with a small avalanche of checks and cash donations to be used for Penny. In fact, we received enough money to replace the food and gifts stolen from Penny and also help a second family in distress.

Over the Christmas break, I recalled the warm generosity of

our new GM partners many times. We can count on them, I realized. They have become part of our extended family; when we need help, when we are in trouble, we can count on them for support, no questions asked. What a wonderful realization at that time of the year.

I was so happy when they had asked what they could do for me in return for speaking at their leadership session, I had not accepted a check from them but asked instead for their involvement.

Barry heard someone in GM's Ontario zone refer to our school as "the Saturn of the education world," meaning of course the innovative and non-conforming approach that GM's Saturn division had become known for.

I was thinking of that remark when I spoke at a celebration of the school's eightieth birthday a few weeks later. Over six hundred visitors crowded the school and grounds, overflowing from the classrooms into the halls, and out of the halls onto the playground. I mentioned the comparison during my talk. "Actually," I quipped, "Saturn is the South Simcoe of the automotive industry."

We both made our points.

The CBC *Man Alive* documentary was aired on a number of occasions, and the day following a repeat telecast, someone commented that our story would make an ideal feature for *Reader's Digest* magazine. "If it's meant to happen, it will," I said.

Obviously, it *was* meant to happen. The previous evening, a woman in Kamloops, B.C., named Lynn Schuyler, was having difficulty dropping off to sleep and thought perhaps a few minutes staring at her TV set might make her drowsy. What she began watching did not make her drowsy at all. It was the *Man Alive* telecast, and instead of preparing her for bed, the show alerted her to a perfect story idea for *Reader's Digest*. The next morning, Lynn began tracking me down, contacting me barely two hours after my off-the-cuff response to the idea of a *Reader's Digest* article on South Simcoe. When Lynn introduced herself and the reason for her call, I burst into laughter. I have always believed that if you are on the right path (or in the flow), the right people will appear and the right things will happen. Not surprisingly, Lynn's telephone call cemented that belief more firmly than ever in my heart.

I was invited to make an appearance on the CBC's immensely popular radio show *Morningside,* hosted by the legendary Peter Gzowski. Peter, besides being perhaps the best-known media celebrity in the country at the time, was also a strong literacy advocate. As the interview progressed, he grew more and more enthusiastic. To demonstrate his support, he said, "Tell me what you need at the school." I asked him what he meant.

"We're being heard by millions of listeners, coast to coast across Canada right now," he said. "If there is something you and the school can use for your programs, go ahead and ask for it."

I was caught off guard. "Wow, Peter, if I knew that you were going to ask me this, I would have made a list; my head has gone blank." I did some quick thinking and asked for two things. Photographs, I explained, played a large role in our work at the school; we displayed photos of our students and their successes throughout the school, as a way of affirming expectations and inspiring them, and we wanted to continue this practice, but there was some expense involved.

Almost immediately, CBC received a call from Anne Hartling, a marketing manager at Kodak. Anne became one of our biggest supporters; not only did she help us with our photography needs, she also visited the school, along with colleagues Sue and Steve, to teach the basics of photography to our students. They learned how to take photos, print them and mount them for display. This evolved into our students taking photos of "what makes me happy." Anne then arranged to have the photos displayed in Shoppers Drug Mart stores. Can you imagine the wonderful feelings that this generated in our community?

I also mentioned how badly we needed a bus from time to time, for field trips that our students could not afford. We wanted our students, many of whom had never travelled beyond their own city limits, to see the neighboring City of Toronto, visit the world famous Niagara Falls, only two hours away, and be exposed to the world beyond their school boundaries.

"Anybody out there got a bus?" Peter said. "Sandra Dean needs a bus!"

A few days later, someone who had been listening to the radio suggested I call the Tim Hortons Coffee Company. Sure enough, they had a bus and were pleased to make it available to us for excursions. Later that school year, our students visited historic sites aboard a luxury air-conditioned bus, thanks to Tim Hortons and Peter Gzowski. Professor Bob Ellis, associate dean at the School of Business at Wilfred Laurier University, asked permission to do a case study on leadership at South Simcoe. He later told me that this case study was a favorite with his students.

The *Reader's Digest* story was one of a long chain of events that spread the South Simcoe Story far beyond our neighborhood. Our story spread across Canada, down to the U.S., then overseas to Europe and eventually all the way to Australia. Strangers began stopping staff members on the street to thank them for the work they were doing. Mail and telephone calls arrived from more foreign locations than I can remember, and requests for interviews and speeches became so numerous that we were unable to handle them all. The flow of letters became so voluminous and time consuming to go through that I had no choice but to place them in a box until someone could find time to read and respond to them. It was reassuring to see such an outpouring of interest, but we could not let it distract us from our prime responsibility, our students.

Just a few years earlier, I had walked in one direction to seek help from the Legion members, and in the other direction looking for assistance from the neighboring mall merchants. Now the traffic had reversed, and as *Together We Light the Way* began making an impact, others were coming to us. It was nothing less than astonishing.

In all, I was interviewed on Peter Gzowski's radio show three times. During one interview, a woman named Courtney Garneau, working in the Federal Justice Department, happened to be listening. The issues of bullying and school violence were beginning to attract wide media interest in Canada, most of it focused on a "Let's get tough with the kids and give them harsher consequences," approach. Our philosophy, of course, had firm consequences for causing harm to others, but we focused heavily on digging deeper, getting to the root cause, and prevention. For us, it was more about helping our students to understand who they were *being* and who they were capable of *becoming*.

Intrigued by this and impressed with our achievements, Courtney telephoned and invited me to a meeting in Ottawa, where I was questioned about our school routines, programs and successes. The Justice officials were all very impressed with our asset based philosophy and by the way we had dramatically reduced bullying, fighting and other forms of violent behavior, by focusing on teaching our students what it meant to be a friend, how to make friends, how to create and maintain healthy, respectful and caring relationships, and how to develop a stronger sense of themselves, who they were and who they were capable of becoming. They were wowed by our simple but powerful methods of gathering data (we had kept statistics on everything we had done from the very beginning); we continuously analyzed our results to learn what was working well and where we should continue to focus our efforts to best help our students.

In later years, I was the only Canadian invited to "testify" and share our ideas and strategies at the White House initiative on Hispanic American Affairs, and it was because we had so many years of data, however simple, to validate our work.

The meeting in Ottawa led to our school district being awarded a grant of over one million dollars to document the *Together We Light the Way* model, developed at South Simcoe, with its routines, strategies and programs, and to then transfer it to other schools across Canada. The model was eventually shared in many places, including India, China, Egypt, Thailand, Brazil, Norway, England, Spain and, of course, the Caribbean.

By my second year, we had already made enormous progress building relationships with the community, boosting the students sense of self-worth and transforming South Simcoe Public School into what was now referred to as the heartbeat of its community, a spiritual oasis for all. We had created a strong foundation for academic excellence.

Unfortunately, factors such as providing breakfast for students, social and emotional learning, community engagement and all the other foundational factors we had focused on, were not measured by the standardized tests in reading, writing and mathematics.

Didn't the test makers realize where we had started and that the task of raising a student's reading level by three or four grade levels is never accomplished overnight? Obviously not!

Our results on the new district-wide exams were dreadful; we lingered at the bottom of the list in every category. Of over a hundred schools in our district, we were dead last.

So much hard work—was it all in vain? No, absolutely not! In my heart, I knew we were on the right track. We had the school statistics to prove it. A high percentage of our students were now attending school regularly and on time, and in-class disturbances had been all but eliminated; therefore, the teachers had more time to focus on the teaching and learning process. Our parents were now making sure that their children were fed and got a good night's sleep, and our students were engaged with their learning—they were smiling, confident and articulate, and they were working hard and said they loved attending school. You could even sense an attitude of striving to learn, everywhere in the school—so many positives.

The staff and I consoled ourselves with this knowledge. But how would our parents react to the disastrous test results? Would they decide that our noble experiment had failed, that their children were doomed to reside at the bottom of the academic totem pole? Should we even discuss the results at the next Parent Rap session? Perhaps we could avoid the subject entirely and hope the question never arose.

We decided to meet the issue head on. At the next Parent

Rap session, I presented the results to our parents and awaited their response. To their everlasting credit, every parent stated flatly that they didn't care about the results of the district-wide exams.

"We know how hard you and your staff are working," one parent said, "and we know that our children are learning—just look at the work they are doing."

"My son is reading, and he used to hate reading," another added. "Now he enjoys it. He's even showing off how well he can read. So what if he's not at the grade three level yet? The way he's going, I know he'll be there by the end of the year. Why don't the testing people recognize what great strides we have made and give us credit for it?"

Our efforts to help our parents understand what we were doing, and asking for their support, were paying off. They knew how much their children had improved, and that they simply needed more time to get to the levels expected on the standardized tests.

Their faith in us was heartwarming, and we all left the session feeling more confident than ever that we were on the right path.

The task ahead was to raise our academic levels. But how?

We gradually restored our confidence. We reviewed our data, strengthened programs where necessary and stayed the course. We also took comfort in the continuing support from officials at the district office, who understood that elevating our academic levels would not be an overnight miracle.

Our director of education, Pauline Laing, persuaded us to apply for an award for Excellence in Business Education Partnerships, from the Conference Board of Canada.

These awards were presented each year to recognize partnerships between schools and businesses; they were highly prized and hotly contested by schools all across the country. If South Simcoe Public School could win recognition in that forum, it would be quite a coup.

With the encouragement and financial support of my director and superintendents, I attended that year's Conference Board event and returned filled with enthusiasm and resolve. South Simcoe, I was convinced, stood a good chance of being selected for recognition at the next event.

The school year was coming to a close, and all the activities, together with the day-to-day demands of my role as principal, were taking a toll on my energy. The truth is, I was growing mentally and physically exhausted. Between acting as principal, supervising programs, maintaining contacts with our community partners and conducting media interviews, my work had become a seemingly endless procession of meetings, discussions and decision making. I usually loved every bit of it, but even happy work can be too much at times. I was paying a price for the long hours and weekend work, even if I refused to admit it.

That summer, both Ishwar and the boys insisted that I take an extended vacation in Trinidad. I had returned to Trinidad frequently to visit my family and friends, who were unfailing in their pride in all that we had accomplished at South Simcoe. But this trip was somewhat special. I spent long hours in conversation with people who had helped shape my values as a child, and the experience was truly a spiritual renewal. Then Ishwar and I went to Tobago, where we had spent our honeymoon so many years earlier, and I whiled away many long, languid days soaking up sunshine, catching up on my sleep, walking on the beaches and generally recharging my batteries.

When I returned to begin the new school year, I discovered a new reservoir of energy, and I applied it towards raising our academic levels to match our other achievements.

More than ever, I appreciated our extended family approach to developing community partnerships. These family members provided a kind of spiritual sustenance to our students, just as my family and friends back in Trinidad had provided for me. I knew that with their assistance, we would succeed.

The school leadership team spent a great deal of time preparing the Conference Board of Canada's award submission. We described our procedures and strategies, recorded our achievements, collated our data and testimonials and evaluated our findings. Many people assisted us, including officials at the district office, who wanted us to succeed.

Then, near disaster. On the day we were to courier our presentation to the Conference Board, to meet the deadline of the following day, we realized that some of the information on the application was inadequate. Rewriting meant missing the one-thirty courier pickup, but we could not send in an inadequate presentation, so we set to work on major revisions. The next pickup time was five-thirty, but by mid-afternoon, we realized we wouldn't make that one either. Tamara, Kim and Pauline searched and found another company that agreed to pick up the presentation at nine o'clock. We worked through the dinner hour, by now practically staggering with exhaustion. Still, we went on; then we even had to cancel that late-hour courier. We finally settled on same-day delivery and found a company that would do this for us for a hefty fee.

We paid the money and somehow also found the energy to wrap things up at eleven o'clock that evening. By that time, our entire bodies were so weary. The next morning, my eyes were still so sore that I couldn't even put my contacts in, and the arrival of the courier service was, quite literally, a sight for sore eyes.

We had all worked so hard, and now everything was in the hands of strangers who, I prayed, would see our work not as some optimistic "love-in" but as a serious, multifaceted and measured effort to reach goals many others had once considered impossible.

The call arrived in February. Tiny South Simcoe Public School, the school that had sat at the very bottom of the Durham District's test results one year earlier, had been declared the best of all Ontario's elementary and secondary schools in the competition for Excellence in Business and Education Partnerships, sponsored by the Conference Board of Canada.

We whooped, we hugged and we laughed. Then I shared the news with the school over the PA system, which set off such an explosion of cheering by the students that I wondered if it could be heard ten miles away, at the school district offices. I followed this up with visits to each classroom, where I explained in detail to the students the meaning of the recognition and why they should feel proud, because the award was more theirs than anyone's.

The national winner would be chosen from among the regional winners at the formal presentation, which was to be held in Saint John, New Brunswick, later in the spring, and this posed a problem. The Conference Board would make travel arrangements for me to attend, but I felt it would be terribly unfair if I were the only representative from the school to attend the awards ceremony. None of our achievements would have been possible without the hard work and sacrifice by the staff, and the support of our partners; they deserved to share the honor and recognition. A team effort had won the award, and a team should be on hand to receive it.

In a meeting with Pauline, I explained my dilemma and made an impulsive promise. "If you can arrange to make time available for the teachers to attend," I said, "I'll arrange the rest." Meaning, of course, the expense of flying our entire staff to New Brunswick.

Pauline came to the rescue. If the parents agreed, a Professional Development Day could be shifted, providing the time needed. The parents enthusiastically supported the idea. Now it was time to raise the money to cover travel and accommodation.

The community support was nothing less than inspirational. When word spread that we needed funds to send the staff to New Brunswick, parents and trustees went to work, and soon contributions of five, ten and twenty-five dollars began arriving, along with congratulations and fervent beliefs that we would be selected best in the country. Substantial amounts came from surprising sources: The neighboring Kmart, where a few years earlier some of our students were considered rampant shoplifters, sent a thousand dollars, while Mike Nicholson, our school trustee, drummed up support from the entire board and even convinced Doug Ross, another trustee, to contribute five hundred dollars.

We invited all our partners to attend, including members of the police force, and the chief of police responded by sending Colin Shaw and his partner in a brand new police van to drive the nine hundred kilometers from Oshawa to Saint John.

The event was much more than an awards ceremony. Each regional winner set up booths and displays in a conference hall where over six hundred attendees, most of them educators, milled about looking at photographs, examining records and chatting with representatives at the booths. Constable Shaw helped at our booth, which drew a few curious comments from visitors, who may have thought a uniformed police officer was an unnecessary player in all our activities.

Everyone seemed intrigued by our programs and impressed with our results. They loved the photographs of the students, which decorated our booth (provided by Anne, Steve and Sue), and they were impressed by the community partnerships we had created. Still, none of us dared to hope that we might be chosen as the winner from all the schools in Canada.

Then the moment for the formal announcement arrived. We held our breath...crossed our fingers...then erupted in more joy and noise than I ever expected a small group of teachers and two police officers could express.

When the pandemonium settled down, I wanted everyone who supported us back home to hear the news. The school district, I knew, was holding an evening meeting; we had to call them and share the excitement. But no one was at the building's main switchboard at that late hour. There was simply no way to get the word to the meeting room—until Constable Shaw said, "Leave it to me." He called police headquarters back in Oshawa and had a police cruiser dispatched, complete with flashing lights, to the board office, where the officer managed to rouse someone who then admitted him to the meeting room, where he shared the good news.

I have always wished in some small way that I had been present that evening when the Durham District School Board, probably deep in a discussion of budgets and curricula, was suddenly interrupted by a police officer arriving with, I'm sure they expected, news of some near or imminent disaster—only to discover that South Simcoe Public had just won a prestigious national award.

The Conference Board of Canada's award was not the first that South Simcoe had ever received, but it was, after all, a national award, and the first from *outside the school system.* It validated all our work with the community; it recognized how much we had accomplished with our limited resources, and proved that *simple* did not mean *simplistic*— our community had stepped up and accepted their social responsibility. "Education is everybody's business," wasn't an empty saying in this neighborhood. They had worked shoulder to shoulder with us to form a healthy, safe and caring protective circle around "our kids." Shouldn't this be something that every school could expect from its community?

Groups of educators began to arrive to learn from us, and it seemed as if everyone was trying to figure out what made us tick. My friend and mentor Ken Leithwood conducted an academic study to see if staff enthusiasm was related to student success, and he surveyed a number of schools, including ours. The results from South Simcoe, he told me with astonishment, went right off the chart; enthusiasm levels were so high that they unfairly skewed the data obtained from other schools in the study—oops!

Things had certainly changed at South Simcoe Public School. Now, we all loved being there.

The children enjoyed the growing attention being paid to them by visitors. Little Meagan, whose singing voice stirred hearts at every school assembly, seemed to take special pride in welcoming visitors. She would rush to greet them, thrust out a tiny hand and say, "Welcome to South Simcoe!" Her positive attitude and her pride in her achievements were obvious—it took only the barest hint to encourage Meagan to display her personal portfolio, which documented all her accomplishments. Meagan was a wonderful example of what could be achieved with encouragement, support and assurance that you are safe, accepted and appreciated.

Meagan's family situation was challenging; she felt no love and appreciation there. Many children react to this kind of situation with rebellion and alienation. But Meagan chose to focus on the acceptance she experienced from her teachers, and later from visitors to the school. Some visitors arrived as skeptical strangers, but they usually departed the school totally beguiled by this little girl's poise, enthusiasm and confidence.

That summer, we were asked to do a presentation at a huge conference in Toronto. It was a big deal to be invited to speak to so many educators, and since we were taking time to do this during our holidays, we decided to go by stretch limousine, complete with uniformed chauffeur, to drive us there and back. On the way back, we toasted our new celebrity status with nonalcoholic champagne!

Even our lovely gardens were attracting attention—the following month, South Simcoe School was declared the winner of the Looking Good Award, given to the school judged to have the most attractive grounds of all the schools in the region. But good looks, visitors and presentations, I kept reminding myself, could only take us so far. Our bottom-of-the-barrel rating for reading, writing and mathematics still felt like a millstone around my neck.

I was comforted by two things: one, we had no direction to go but up; and two, our own school results demonstrated that we were making steady academic progress. Our standing in the district tests did not capture the reality at South Simcoe.

By the time the Ontario Ministry of Education announced that it would conduct a provincial standardized test, we knew that we would have better results. Sally Roberts and Joanne Blohm, the grade three teachers, were confident in the abilities of their students. The tests were administered in the spring, and when several months later the results finally arrived, the entire staff gathered in the staff room to hear the news.

It was amazing. South Simcoe Public School was no longer at the bottom of the barrel, or even in the middle of the pack. Our results were substantially higher than the average for all elementary schools in the entire province of Ontario. We had managed to rise dramatically in the ratings for reading, writing and mathematics. The gardens, the awards, the recognition and the media coverage all paled in comparison. South Simcoe students were not only more proud, more confident, more respectful and more articulate than ever before—they were also academically outstanding!

What strategies do you use to encourage an
asset-based mindset in your school?
To find out how success mapping can help you improve
your asset-based system, visit my website:
APublicSchoolMiracle.com.

Chapter 12

The Gifts They Gave Us

Throughout 1996, South Simcoe garnered international recognition. Early that year, we were informed that Michael Fullan, who at that time was the dean of the Faculty of Education at the University of Toronto, had nominated our school district as an entry in a competition to honor excellence in school systems, sponsored by the giant Bertelsmann Foundation of Germany. Although the nomination process stated that only one school should represent the district and be visited by the judges, Michael included South Simcoe Public School as a second school, stating that it was an example of great change made with very few resources.

The criteria for the competition required the jury to assess a long list of qualities, including each school system's concern for learning and life chances, originality and evolution, employee potential, innovative school leadership, participation of pupils, parents and other agencies, co-operation between individual schools and external decision makers, evaluation and quality assurance, and a framework to support similar development on a national level.

We readied the school for the visit from the Bertelsmann judges, and added a few extra touches. The judges' visit included the lunch hour, and we were asked to recommend a restaurant for them. When we learned that they would be touring other schools all over the world for three months before arriving at South Simcoe, we decided that instead of recommending a restaurant to them, we would prepare a special home cooked meal for them—we figured by this point, they were probably growing tired of restaurant meals.

Alvena, a super chef when it came to baking, made fresh bread, and its heavenly aroma wafted towards the judges as they entered the building; Jane cooked and served her favorite casserole, and we all contributed to dessert. We invited Phil Lawson, our Swiss Chalet partner, and Curt Tingley from General Motors, to talk about our partnerships and discuss our successes from the perspective of community partners.

Before they began their tour of the classrooms, we explained our asset-based philosophy, our agreements-based behavioral approach and our academic strategies, and we showed them how we collectively gathered and analyzed data.

The judges went from classroom to classroom, growing more impressed by the minute. In Sally Roberts' grade four class, they inspected the student portfolios and asked one girl to name her best subject.

"Reading," she said without hesitation. "I'm a really good reader."

One member asked how she could tell.

"Easy," the girl replied. "I'll show you."

As the judges watched, she withdrew her portfolio from the desk, opened it up and showed them graphs that illustrated her level of reading in September and her current level. The girl had progressed three years in reading levels in less than one year, and she demonstrated it with poise and pride.

Downstairs in the kindergarten class, Nancy was reading a story to her students when the judges entered. After the judges introduced themselves, one asked the students if they were proud of their school. "Yes!" the children responded, almost rattling the windows with their voices.

"You show them," Nancy suggested to the class, and the youngsters spontaneously exploded in the loudest, most enthusiastic South Simcoe Chant ever delivered by a group of five-year-olds.

At the end of the tour, the jury members expressed their surprise and pleasure at the staff's enthusiasm and dedication, and at the confidence and pride of the students. They also went on to praise the consistency of our programming. "In every classroom," one of them commented, "from kindergarten to grade eight, the teachers and students are clear about their guiding principles, the goals of the school, their classroom goals and their personal goals. They can clearly articulate the agreements they have made about speaking and behaving in a respectful manner. They can also describe to you how they work to develop respectful relationships.

"What's more, teachers have portfolios divided into the areas of professional growth and personal development. Students' portfolios are divided into the areas of academic growth and personal development, with demonstrations of their growth and development as individuals, their social and emotional learning, teamwork and leadership, how they have participated in the leadership process, how they have taken charge without being asked and how they use their strengths and capabilities to make improvements. They can describe the strategies they used to help them to succeed, and they can demonstrate how they measure their progress. The most significant point is that they are consistently achieving the goals they set for themselves."

The judges were impressed—so impressed that a film crew arrived from Germany, in May, to spend two days filming at our school, and an additional two days at Sinclair Secondary School, the "showcase school" for the award. The presence of the film crew was evidence that we had done more than simply impress the Bertelsmann judges; and in September, it was made official: Durham District School Board, represented by Sinclair Secondary School, with South Simcoe Public School also showcased, had won out over school systems in Hungary, New Zealand, Norway, Scotland and Switzerland, to be declared the best, most innovative school system in the world.

Linda Scott, from the Conference Board of Canada, asked us to host a group of visitors attending an International Partnership Conference in Toronto. Since we were the previous year's winner, a number of people wanted to visit our school. I watched as one visitor, Ola Risnes, a stern looking Norwegian, moved through the school taking videos of everything, without exhibiting any apparent response to all that he saw and heard. I feared he actually disapproved of our programs, or was disappointed in some way, but later that year, when I encountered him at an educational conference in Calgary, I learned that he had, in fact, been very impressed. I also discovered he was head of the Norwegian Confederation of Business and Industry. As a result of his visit and that meeting, I was invited to make the keynote address at the International Partnership Conference, in Norway, the following summer.

Other invitations began arriving from international destinations. I was delighted to be invited by the Royal Bank in Trinidad and Tobago to return to my home country, where I spoke about the development of business and educational partnerships. The Prime Minister opened the event and, needless to say, the experience was immensely flattering to the entire South Simcoe family.

For me, in many ways, it was like coming full circle. It enabled me to reach back to my roots, to the region and the culture that had shaped me, and shaped so much of what happened at South

Simcoe School. Shortly afterwards, the Prime Minister of Grenada invited me to Grenada to launch a partnership initiative with school principals, teachers and business people. I made several visits to Grenada to do this, all funded by Rob Pitfield from Scotiabank.

During this time, we created the Prime Minister's Awards for Excellence in Business Education Partnerships. After the ceremonies, I was invited to address the Prime Ministers of the other Caribbean nations. Shortly afterwards, I set off for Jamaica to speak to Scotiabank managers at their annual leadership training conference.

After the South African elections, I was invited to Durban to give the keynote address to a conference centered on the importance of the community supporting students and their education. The people I met in South Africa, where there was such hunger for knowledge and so few resources to provide it at the time, were thrilled to hear the *Together We Light the Way* message. They liked the idea that a small school, facing many challenges in far-off Canada, had an asset-based philosophy and succeeded in spite of limited resources, by creating cost-effective and innovative programs, and working with their community. If we could do it, I assured them, they could as well.

I stressed the need to believe in children and support them as they learned how to believe in themselves; to believe that they have strengths and capabilities, and to work with them to guide them to inner wisdom, and discover those strengths, nurture them and then use them to improve their own situations as well as their communities. I explained that with the support of business and community partners, all this was possible.

"Not support from their wallets," I emphasized. "Support from their hearts." I explained how a large number of caring and concerned individuals, each giving just a little of their time, made an enormous impact on the lives of our students and encouraged them to develop their own partnerships.

I described the struggles faced by students such as Melanie, Meagan, Bobby, Leonard, Cathy, Barbara and so many others we had encountered, and how we taught them strategies to help them cope, while supporting them as they grew more and more resilient.

I affirmed what they all knew, that easy solutions rarely exist to the significant problems faced by mankind.

I closed my presentation with the thought, "If we can work together to help our children change the way they think about themselves, feel about themselves and see themselves, we will change their lives for the better."

One day in the spring of 1998, I returned home from school as usual and checked my voicemail system. All but one were the familiar kinds of messages, spoken in familiar voices by people with familiar names.

One was anonymous. I could not recognize the voice. "Sandra," it said, "I'm someone who cares about South Simcoe

School, and I want you to know this. The school is going be closed. I don't want you to be shocked by the news, because I know you have said that it would only close over your dead body."

That was all. They hung up. I felt as though I had been kicked in the stomach.

It could have been just a crank call. Who would leave a message like that without mentioning their name? But the words had been delivered with such authority that I knew they were true. Due to budget restraints, school boards everywhere were being forced to reassess the economics of operating buildings that were old and costly to maintain.

Like South Simcoe.

I didn't mention the telephone call to anyone.

A few days later, when I was at the board offices, hoping against hope that the rumor was untrue, Grant Yeo, my director, called me into his office for a chat. He closed the door behind us, and I knew instinctively what he was going to say.

"We're going to be announcing the closure of your school," he said in a solemn yet kind and caring voice, like a physician announcing the death of a relative. "I want to handle this in a manner that won't create a negative impact on the community, and I need your co-operation."

Thanks to the anonymous telephone call, I managed to remain calm while he explained that, in a sweeping cost-cutting plan, the Durham District School Board would be closing eleven older schools, most of them in heavily urbanized areas, and constructing twelve new ones in developing neighborhoods.

It was not something anyone wanted to do, but every possible way of keeping the school open had been explored. There was no real alternative. Grant encouraged me to look on the bright side of things. I had always despaired that South Simcoe lacked a gymnasium, a large library and sufficient washrooms. Moving the students to a newer, larger school would provide them with all of these facilities.

I tried, but I simply couldn't accept the closing of South Simcoe as a step forward for the students.

Things grew worse when, soon after my talk with the director, I had to sit through a meeting and listen as someone read aloud the names of all the schools to be closed. Through the list they went, moving closer to the revelation that I knew was coming but found difficult to acknowledge, and when they reached "South Simcoe Public School," it was as though someone plunged a knife into my heart.

I sat frozen in my chair. I may have been a dedicated educational professional and a member of this important and influential group, but I was blinking back tears. How could this be the fate of a school that was praised as a beacon of hope for other schools—that helped the district win an international award and was described as a spiritual oasis for its community?

When the meeting finally ended, I managed to rise from my chair, walk to my car, drive the long distance back to the school and break the sad news to the staff. By this time, I had resigned myself to reality. Drawing on my leadership training, I began concentrating on ways to help the staff and students deal with the news.

At the school, I had to take the official board position, explaining the logic of its decision to the hardest-working, most dedicated group of teachers I had ever been privileged to know, while they dabbed tissues at their eyes or stared blankly into space. "This is not entirely unexpected," I pointed out. "We have done wonderful things here, and made a difference to so many students. Unfortunately, the building is old; it is inefficient and very expensive for the district to operate, and there is no room for expansion and building a proper gymnasium, library or other things we need." I asked them to be strong and work together to make the change as easy as possible for our students.

In June, the day before our Community Celebration Day, and also the celebration of the school's eighty-second anniversary, the decision was made public. At the end of the next school year, South Simcoe Public School would be closed and shuttered, left to await demolition or sale. The press stormed the school in the middle of the festivities, with five TV stations dispatching cameras and reporters to cover the story. Fortunately, I had anticipated the media response. Roger Morin—one of our most dedicated and hardworking parents, someone who worked with and supported me throughout my last years at South Simcoe— along with Ann Hartling and Linda Sinclair, helped me prepare a statement regarding the closing of the school, and I read it over and over again to reporters and interviewers throughout the day. The joy of the celebration, of course, dissolved in the reality of the school's imminent closing.

That's one reason I remember the day so vividly. The other reason? It was the only time in all my years at South Simcoe that we had rain on the school's Community Celebration Day.

With the word now made official, I personally visited each class, explaining to the students that they deserved better facilities than we were able to provide at South Simcoe. It was a fine old building, but its time as a school had passed. "Nobody enjoys closing a school," I said, "least of all its principal." Least of all *this* principal, I might have added.

And that October, in the midst of a beautiful autumn, the final autumn in the final year for South Simcoe Public School, a remarkable thing happened.

Once again, standardized tests had been conducted to determine abilities in reading, writing and mathematics. This time, we didn't open the results with the same breathless excitement as before; but we were stunned, nevertheless. The findings were clear and unequivocal: South Simcoe students were performing at the top levels in reading, writing and mathematics; in fact, 94 percent of our students achieved the top levels. South Simcoe was no longer merely above average in its academic performance; on the basis of these tests, it was the most successful inner-city school in the entire province.

There was more.

According to a district report, a remarkably high percentage of South Simcoe students attended school regularly and on time, and the overwhelming majority of our grade seven and grade eight students earned at least two A's on their report card. Once notorious for incidents of vandalism and shoplifting, the report noted, South Simcoe now enjoyed the steady support of twenty-six business partners and community agencies. And the school that once could entice only three parents to each Parent Rap session, now drew at least one out of every four parents to its meetings.

Upon hearing the news of the school's closing, some of these same parents resolved to save the building. Their presentations, letters to the editors of local newspapers and outraged telephone calls to local politicians all repeated the same theme: How could they close a school that had won all these national and international awards? They can't just shut down a school that had done so much for so many in the South Simcoe neighborhood.

Well, they could, and they did.

Towards the end of 1998, I had accepted the decision intellectually, if not emotionally, and was determined to handle the situation with as much grace and decorum as I could muster. Still, it seemed as though irony kept piling atop irony.

During the same week, in December 1998, that the decision to close South Simcoe Public School was declared binding and irrevocable, the federal justice department announced a spending commitment of $1.8 million to fund the transfer of our programs to schools all across the country, along with a contribution from the Ontario Ministry of Education and Training. This was announced at a Celebrating Our Stars ceremony, at the Legion Hall, and was attended by a host of federal members of parliament and members of the provincial legislature, plus several business and community partners. It was a huge celebration. Every staff member, every student and every interested parent we could squeeze into the hall was invited to attend. I reminded each class that they had not only bettered themselves by the work they had done at South Simcoe, but they had also provided a model for others all over the world.

I was asked to head the justice department's initiative to transfer the *Together We Light the Way* model; the project was called, *"Creating Safe and Caring Learning Communities."* Yes, *Together We Light the Way* was now a model. The work we had done, and the lessons we had learned, would now make a difference to untold numbers of students in many Canadian schools and communities. We had helped to make a difference to our school community; now we could perhaps help to make a difference to an entire country, and even beyond Canada.

The ministry's description of our program, as contained in a news release of December 16, 1998, managed to sum up all that we had conceived, refined and practiced over the previous seven years:

Together We Light the Way...*is a school-based intervention model that builds resiliency and responsibility in young children, and relies on the commitment of teachers, parents and the community for its success. The model reduces risk factors affecting young children, and increases protective factors.*

Why would the Ministry of Justice make use of our program?

Because *the elementary school setting provides perhaps the only consistent access to large numbers of children.*

My final day at South Simcoe fell immediately before the Christmas vacation period. During my years at South Simcoe, we maintained a tradition at the school, of "clapping out" grade eights who were moving on to high school. On their final day at the school, the grade eights would walk the long corridor and down the front steps, which was lined with all the other students. As the senior students made their final exit, the remaining students would shake their hands and applaud them. This was our "clap out," and it proved so moving and popular that some grade eights would exit and scurry around to re-enter the school from the other side, just to be "clapped out" again.

I had always dreamed of leaving in the same manner. But it would be both inappropriate and too emotional. So there was no clapping out for me. My final day ended with the usual rush of telephone calls, a raft of documents to be signed and a long walk, alone down the hall and out the door.

During this walk, I considered something that I had not given much thought to in the past. Our aim had been to make South

Simcoe a safe, caring and healthy place to learn, grow and develop—a spiritual refuge as it were—for our students. We had achieved all that we had planned to; our students knew that they were loved, respected and cared for within its shabby old walls.

Yet, over my last few years there, I felt that *I* had been the one who was loved and cared for. If I became sick, someone watched over me; whenever I needed a kind word, someone spoke it for me. I genuinely loved the school, the staff, the students, the community and all that they represented. I recognized the changes that had taken place within me. Like the students, I too had grown and developed. Like them, I had discovered an inner strength I never knew I possessed. I had become more centered and grounded as a person, and much more resilient.

I am forever grateful. The physician, in seeking to heal and care for her patients, found herself also healed and cared for from the same process.

I did not, and still don't, enjoy goodbyes. So that night, filled with a maelstrom of emotions, and recalling all that the school meant to me, I got into my car and drove home.

Times and situations change. Teachers and students alike must understand and accept this fact of life. When I had been assigned to South Simcoe, it was a place to which I didn't want to go; now it was a place I didn't want to leave. Life certainly does work in mysterious ways.

One of the foundations of wisdom, I believe, is the awareness of universal themes, concepts of belief that are equally valid everywhere in the world. Among the most important of these universal themes is the one my father had first taught me when I accompanied him on his visits to distant villages, seeking people who needed assistance.

Believe in yourself and others. Understand who you are and what you stand for. Believe that you have the gifts, talents, capabilities and strength within you to make a positive difference in the world. Act with kindness and compassion, and help others to see opportunities in their challenges. Then support them as they face and deal with these challenges; and as they grow more confident in their abilities, they will discover new opportunities for themselves. Then they will assume the role you had undertaken earlier, and they too will help others to see opportunities in their challenges—and so the cycle continues.

Respect yourself and others is another theme. I believe every family, every community, every society should nurture this concept in its children. We all have the right to be respected, and with that right comes the responsibility to respect others. Know this, and let this thought guide your behavior to be kind, compassionate and caring. Remember that everything you do— every word, every small gesture, every act you perform—creates a ripple and affects others. Creating, maintaining and sustaining respectful, caring and loving relationships throughout life will develop strength of character.

Be inclusive and give hope to others. This may be the most valuable universal theme of all. With being included and given hope, children embrace a vision of better things for themselves, and realize that they do not have to settle for the same conditions into which they were born. They can rise from their circumstances and, with support from others, create a life of their dreams

We gave the students of South Simcoe a realization of the vast opportunities available to them in life, an awareness of the gifts, talents and capabilities that they carried within themselves, and the knowledge that there is always a way—they just had to persevere and find it. We were all there to support them on their journey. They gave themselves better grades, a more promising future and a sense of the unlimited potential within them. The things they gave my staff and me are beyond measure and description.

I will always treasure the South Simcoe experience!

What strategies do you have in place to educate the whole child and ensure that they achieve harmony of heart, mind, spirit and intellect?
If you want to learn additional proven strategies to educate the whole child, visit my website: APublicSchoolMiracle.com.

www.ingramcontent.com/pod-product-compliance
Lightning Source LLC
Chambersburg PA
CBHW060002100426
42740CB00010B/1373